Now & Later

160
Hearty Recipes that Turn One Meal into Two

About Weight Watchers

Weight Watchers International, Inc. is the world's leading provider of weight management services, operating globally through a network of Company-owned and franchise operations. Weight Watchers holds over 48,000 weekly meetings, where members receive group support and education about healthful eating patterns, behavior modification, and physical activity. Weight-loss and weight-management results vary by individual. We recommend that you attend Weight Watchers meetings to benefit from the supportive environment you'll find there and follow the comprehensive Weight Watchers program, which includes food plans, an activity plan, and a thinking-skills plan. In addition, Weight Watchers offers a wide range of products, publications and programs for those interested in weight loss and weight control. For the Weight Watchers meeting nearest you, call 800-651-6000. For information on bringing Weight Watchers to your workplace, call **800-8AT-WORK.** Also, visit us at our Web site, **WeightWatchers.com,** or look for *Weight Watchers Magazine* at your newsstand or in your meeting room.

SWEET POTATO FALAFEL
SANDWICHES, PAGE 157

WEIGHT WATCHERS PUBLISHING GROUP

EDITORIAL DIRECTOR	**NANCY GAGLIARDI**
CREATIVE DIRECTOR	**ED MELNITSKY**
PRODUCTION MANAGER	**ALAN BIEDERMAN**
PHOTO EDITOR	**DEBORAH HARDT**
MANAGING EDITOR	**SARAH WHARTON**
EDITORIAL ASSISTANT	**CELIA SHATZMAN**
FOOD EDITOR	**EILEEN RUNYAN**
EDITORS	**JACKIE MILLS, CAROL PRAGER**
NUTRITION CONSULTANT	**U. BEATE KRINKE**
COVER PHOTOGRAPHER	**RITA MAAS**
COVER FOOD STYLIST	**ANNE DISRUDE**
COVER PROP STYLIST	**CATHY COOK**
PHOTOGRAPHER	**PHILIP FRIEDMAN**
FOOD STYLIST	**SUSAN VAJARANANT**
PROP STYLIST	**LAURENT LABORIE**
ART DIRECTOR	**DANIELA HRITCU**

ON THE COVER: Baked Pasta and Meatballs, page 106 and Sicilian Meatball Soup, page 107

About Our Recipes

We make every effort to ensure that you will have success with our recipes. For best results and for nutritional accuracy, please keep these guidelines in mind:

• Recipes in this book have been developed for members who are following the **Momentum™** plan. We include *POINTS* ® values for every recipe. *POINTS* values are assigned based on calories, fat (grams), and fiber (grams) provided for a serving size of a recipe.

• All recipes feature approximate nutritional information; our recipes are analyzed for Calories (Cal), Total Fat (Fat), Saturated Fat (Sat Fat), Trans Fat (Trans Fat), Cholesterol (Chol), Sodium (Sod), Carbohydrates (Carb), Dietary Fiber (Fib), Protein (Prot), and Calcium (Calc).

• Nutritional information for recipes that include meat, poultry, and fish are based on cooked skinless boneless portions (unless otherwise stated), with the fat trimmed.

• We recommend that you buy lean meat and poultry, then trim it of all visible fat before cooking. When poultry is cooked with the skin on, we suggest removing the skin before eating.

• Before serving, divide foods—including any vegetables, sauce, or accompaniments—into portions of equal size according to the designated number of servings per recipe.

• Any substitutions made to the ingredients will alter the "Per serving" nutritional information and may affect the *POINTS* value.

• All fresh fruits, vegetables, and greens in recipes should be rinsed before using.

• All ◈™ Filling Extra suggestions have a *POINTS* value of *0* unless otherwise stated.

• Recipes that work with the Simply Filling technique are listed on page 191.

contents

chapter 1
Beef and More 8

chapter 2
Poultry Plus 52

chapter 3
Pasta! Pasta! 92

chapter 4
Take it Slow 118

chapter 5
Go Vegetarian 142

chapter 1
Beef and More

Spiced Steak with Onions and Peppers 10
French Dip Sandwiches 11

Asian-Style Grilled Flank Steak 12
Negamaki with Ginger Dipping Sauce 13

Tandoori Beef Kebabs 14
Easy Beef Curry 15

Beef Burgundy Stew 16
Beef Stroganoff 17

Chimichurri Pepper Steak 18
Speedy Beef Fajitas 19

Pressure-Cooker Corned Beef 20
Corned Beef Hash 21

Smoky Beef Tacos 22
Beef and Bean Sloppy Joes 23

Hoisin Burgers 24
Korean Beef in Lettuce Cups 25

Old-Fashioned Meatloaf 26
Italian Wedding Soup 27

Beef in Tomato-Ginger Sauce 28
Lebanese Pita Pizzas 29

Double Chili Pork Roast 30
Pork and Bok Choy Noodle Bowl 31

Chipotle Roast Pork 32
Mexican Pork and Veggie Bake 33

Salsa Verde Pork Stew 34
Pork Tostadas 35

Orange-Glazed Pork Chops with Fennel 36
Lemony Pork and Lentil Salad 37

Miso-Glazed Pork 38
Pork Fried Rice 39

Balsamic Sausage and Peppers 40
Sausage Shepherd's Pie 41

Ham with Fresh Peach Chutney 42
Ham and Apple Slaw 43

Roast Lamb with Bulgur and Mint Pesto 44
Lamb Tagine with Apricots 45

Lamb and Vegetable Stew 46
Lamb-Noodle Casserole 47

Veal Stew Marsala 48
Savory Stuffed Acorn Squash 49

Veal Saltimbocca 50
Saltimbocca Fennel and Orange Salad 51

Spiced Steak with Onions and Peppers

prep 15 MIN • **grill/cook** 25 MIN • **serves** 4 PLUS LEFTOVERS

1 tablespoon coarsely ground black pepper	2 teaspoons olive oil
1 tablespoon ground coriander	2 large sweet onions, thinly sliced
2 teaspoons ground allspice	1 large red bell pepper, thinly sliced
1 teaspoon kosher salt	1 large green bell pepper, thinly sliced
1 (2-pound) top round steak, about 1 inch thick, trimmed	¼ cup water

1 Spray the grill rack with nonstick spray and prepare a medium hot fire.

2 Mix the black pepper, coriander, allspice, and ½ teaspoon of the salt in a small bowl; transfer 1½ teaspoons of the spice mixture to a cup and reserve. Rub the remaining spice mixture on both sides of the steak.

3 Place the steak on the grill rack and grill, until an instant-read thermometer inserted into the side of the steak registers 145°F for medium, 7–8 minutes on each side. Transfer to a cutting board and cover loosely with foil. Let stand 5 minutes.

4 Meanwhile, heat the oil in a large skillet over medium-high heat. Add the onions and the reserved spice mixture; cook, stirring occasionally, until the onions are golden brown, about 12 minutes. Stir in the bell peppers, water, and the remaining ½ teaspoon of salt. Cover and cook until the bell peppers are just tender and the liquid evaporates, 6 minutes.

5 Cut the steak crosswise in half. Transfer 1½ cups of the vegetables and half of the steak to a container and let cool. Cover and refrigerate up to 3 days for later use in French Dip Sandwiches, opposite. Cut the remaining half of steak across the grain into 12 slices. Serve with the remaining 2 cups of vegetables.

PER SERVING (3 slices steak with ½ cup vegetables): 181 Cal, 5 g Fat, 1 g Sat Fat, 0 g Trans Fat, 61 mg Chol, 271 mg Sod, 8 g Carb, 2 g Fib, 26 g Prot, 30 mg Calc. ***POINTS*** value: **4.**

French Dip Sandwiches

prep 10 MIN · grill/cook 10 MIN · serves 4

1   cup low-sodium beef broth

1½ cups reserved cooked vegetables and 1 pound reserved cooked steak from Spiced Steak with Onions and Peppers (opposite)

4   (3-ounce) multigrain rolls, split

1 Bring the broth to a boil in a large skillet. Add the vegetables, reduce the heat, and simmer.

2 Meanwhile, thinly slice the steak. Add the steak to the skillet, stir to mix, and simmer until heated through, 5 minutes. With a slotted spoon, divide the steak and vegetables evenly on the bottoms of the rolls. Cover with the tops of the rolls to make 4 sandwiches. Serve with the pan juices for dipping.

PER SERVING (1 sandwich with 3 tablespoons pan juices): 276 Cal, 6 g Fat, 2 g Sat Fat, 0 g Trans Fat, 61 mg Chol, 335 mg Sod, 24 g Carb, 3 g Fib, 31 g Prot, 78 mg Calc. *POINTS* value: **5.**

◆ Filling Extra

Serve either the Spiced Steak with Onions and Peppers or the French Dip Sandwiches with 4 cups of your favorite mixed salad greens tossed with 1 tablespoon balsamic vinegar and salt and black pepper to taste.

make this...
Asian-Style Grilled Flank Steak

prep 10 MIN • **grill** 15 MIN • **serves** 4 PLUS LEFTOVERS

¼ cup low-sodium soy sauce

2 tablespoons rice vinegar or white-wine vinegar

2 tablespoons mild cayenne pepper sauce

1 tablespoon packed brown sugar

2 tablespoons chopped peeled fresh ginger

2 garlic cloves, chopped

1 (2-pound) flank steak, trimmed

1 tablespoon hoisin sauce

1 Mix the soy sauce, vinegar, pepper sauce, brown sugar, ginger, and garlic in a zip-close plastic bag; add the steak. Squeeze out the air and seal the bag; turn to coat the steak. Refrigerate, turning the bag occasionally, at least 2 hours or overnight.

2 Spray the grill rack with nonstick spray and prepare a medium hot fire. Place the steak on the grill rack and grill until an instant-read thermometer inserted into the side of the steak registers 145°F for medium, 8–9 minutes on each side. Transfer the steak to a cutting board and cover loosely with foil. Let stand 5 minutes.

3 Cut the steak crosswise in two. Wrap and refrigerate half of the steak up to 3 days for later use in Negamaki with Ginger Dipping Sauce, opposite. Brush the remaining half of the steak with the hoisin sauce and cut across the grain into 12 slices.

PER SERVING (3 slices): 196 Cal, 5 g Fat, 2 g Sat Fat, 0 g Trans Fat, 83 mg Chol, 196 mg Sod, 3 g Carb, 0 g Fib, 33 g Prot, 6 mg Calc. **POINTS** value: **4.**

◆ Filling Extra

Add a few scallions to the grill rack and grill 2-3 minutes, turning occasionally, to serve with the steak.

...then this! Negamaki with Ginger Dipping Sauce

prep 25 MIN · cook 10 MIN · serves 4

- **24** pencil-thin fresh asparagus, trimmed
- **2** carrots, cut into 24 matchstick-thin strips
- **¼** cup low-sodium soy sauce
- **2** tablespoons seasoned rice vinegar
- **1** teaspoon grated peeled fresh ginger

- **½** teaspoon Asian (dark) sesame oil
- **1** pound reserved cooked steak from Asian-Style Grilled Flank Steak (opposite), cut into 24 slices
- **2** teaspoons toasted sesame seeds (optional)

1 Bring a large saucepan of lightly salted water to a boil. Add the asparagus and carrots; cook until crisp-tender, 3 minutes. Drain. Rinse under cold water until cool and drain.

2 Meanwhile, to make the dipping sauce, mix the soy sauce, vinegar, ginger, and sesame oil in a cup. Gently pound each slice of the steak to 1/16-inch thickness with a meat mallet or heavy saucepan.

3 Working with 1 slice of the steak at a time, put 1 piece each of the asparagus and carrot crosswise at the end nearest you. Roll up jelly-roll style to make a total of 24 negamaki. Sprinkle evenly with the sesame seeds (if using). Serve with the dipping sauce.

PER SERVING (6 negamaki with scant 2 tablespoons dipping sauce without sesame seeds): 247 Cal, 5 g Fat, 2 g Sat Fat, 0 g Trans Fat, 83 mg Chol, 806 mg Sod, 12 g Carb, 3 g Fib, 36 g Prot, 36 mg Calc. **POINTS** value: **5.**

make this... Tandoori Beef Kebabs

prep 20 MIN · grill 10 MIN · serves 4 PLUS LEFTOVERS

½   cup plain fat-free yogurt
2   tablespoons apple-cider vinegar
2   tablespoons grated peeled fresh ginger
4   garlic cloves, finely chopped
1   tablespoon curry powder
1   tablespoon hot pepper sauce

½   teaspoon ground allspice
2   pounds top round steak, trimmed and cut into 24 (1-inch) chunks
1   large green bell pepper, cut into 12 pieces
12   cherry tomatoes
4   large scallions, cut into 1-inch pieces

1 Mix the yogurt, vinegar, ginger, garlic, curry powder, pepper sauce, and allspice in a zip-close plastic bag; add the beef. Squeeze out the air and seal the bag; turn to coat the beef. Refrigerate, turning the bag occasionally, at least 1 hour or up to 3 hours.

2 Spray the grill rack with nonstick spray and prepare a medium hot fire.

3 Meanwhile, alternately thread 12 of the beef chunks, the bell pepper, tomatoes, and scallions on 4 (10-to 12-inch) metal skewers. Thread the remaining 12 beef chunks on 2 (10- to 12-inch) metal skewers. Place the kebabs on the grill rack and grill, until the beef is medium, 5–6 minutes on each side.

4 Remove the steak from the beef kebab skewers; wrap and refrigerate up to 3 days for later use in Easy Beef Curry, opposite. Transfer the remaining beef and vegetable kebabs to a platter.

PER SERVING (1 kebab): 180 Cal, 4 g Fat, 1 g Sat Fat, 0 g Trans Fat, 62 mg Chol, 63 mg Sod, 9 g Carb, 2 g Fib, 27 g Prot, 69 mg Calc. **POINTS** value: **4.**

Easy Beef Curry

prep 15 MIN • cook 15 MIN • serves 4

- **1** cup low-sodium beef broth
- **¾** pound fresh green beans, trimmed and cut into 1-inch pieces
- **1** cup canned chickpeas, rinsed and drained
- **¼** cup all-fruit apricot preserves
- **4** scallions, sliced
- **2** teaspoons curry powder
- **¼** teaspoon salt
- **1** (8.8-ounce) package cooked brown rice (about 1¾ cups)
- **1** pound reserved cooked beef from Tandoori Beef Kebabs (opposite)
- **½** cup low-fat sour cream

1 Bring the broth to a boil in a large skillet. Add the green beans; cover and cook 4 minutes. Stir in the chickpeas, preserves, scallions, curry powder, and salt. Reduce the heat; cover and simmer until the green beans are tender, 4 minutes.

2 Meanwhile, microwave the rice according to the package directions.

3 Add the beef to the skillet; cover and cook until heated through, 3 minutes. Stir in the sour cream and cook, stirring constantly, just until heated through, 1 minute. Serve with the rice.

PER SERVING (1½ cups curry with scant ½ cup rice): 402 Cal, 8 g Fat, 3 g Sat Fat, 0 g Trans Fat, 72 mg Chol, 436 mg Sod, 49 g Carb, 8 g Fib, 35 g Prot, 141 mg Calc. **POINTS** value: **8.**

make this... Beef Burgundy Stew

prep 25 MIN • cook 1 HR 45 MIN • serves 4 PLUS LEFTOVERS

2	pounds bottom round roast, trimmed and cut into ¾-inch chunks
¼	cup all-purpose flour
1	tablespoon olive oil
1	(14½-ounce) can low-sodium beef broth
1	cup dry red wine
1	(16-ounce) package frozen pearl onions
1	(10-ounce) package fresh mushrooms

2	tablespoons tomato paste
4	garlic cloves, sliced
1½	teaspoons dried thyme
½	teaspoon salt
¼	teaspoon black pepper
1	pound carrots, halved lengthwise and thickly sliced

1 Toss the beef and flour in a medium bowl until evenly coated. Heat the oil in a large Dutch oven over medium-high heat. Add the beef, in batches if necessary, and cook, turning occasionally, until browned, about 6 minutes. Transfer to a medium bowl with a slotted spoon.

2 Add the broth, wine, onions, mushrooms, tomato paste, garlic, thyme, salt, and pepper; bring to a boil, scraping up the browned bits from the bottom of the Dutch oven. Stir in the beef and reduce the heat. Cover and simmer 1 hour. Stir in the carrots. Cover and simmer until the beef and vegetables are fork-tender, 30 minutes. Transfer 3 cups of the stew to a container and let cool. Cover and refrigerate up to 4 days for later use in Beef Stroganoff, opposite. Divide the remaining 5 cups of stew among 4 bowls.

PER SERVING (1¼ cups): 359 Cal, 9 g Fat, 3 g Sat Fat, 0 g Trans Fat, 104 mg Chol, 367 mg Sod, 22 g Carb, 4 g Fib, 47 g Prot, 61 mg Calc. **POINTS** value: **7.**

Beef Stroganoff

prep 10 MIN • cook 20 MIN • serves 4

¾ cup whole-wheat orzo	½ cup fat-free sour cream
1 cup water	⅛ teaspoon salt
2 tablespoons all-purpose flour	⅛ teaspoon black pepper
3 cups reserved cooked Beef Burgundy Stew (opposite)	2 tablespoons chopped fresh chives

1 Cook the orzo according to the package directions, omitting the salt if desired.

2 While the orzo is cooking, whisk the water and flour in a glass measuring cup until blended. Bring the stew to a simmer in a large saucepan over medium heat, breaking the beef into small pieces with a wooden spoon. Stir in the flour mixture and cook, stirring frequently, until the mixture returns to a simmer, 2 minutes. Stir in the sour cream, salt, and pepper. Reduce the heat and cook the stroganoff just until heated through, 1 minute.

3 Drain the orzo and transfer to a large bowl; top with the stroganoff and sprinkle with the chives.

PER SERVING (¾ cup stroganoff with about ½ cup orzo): 364 Cal, 6 g Fat, 2 g Sat Fat, 0 g Trans Fat, 66 mg Chol, 424 mg Sod, 44 g Carb, 5 g Fib, 35 g Prot, 92 mg Calc. *POINTS* value: **7.**

◆ Filling Extra

Stir 2 cups frozen peas into the beef mixture with the sour cream in step 2. The per-serving *POINTS* value will increase by *1.*

make this... Chimichurri Pepper Steak

prep 25 MIN • grill 15 MIN • serves 4 PLUS LEFTOVERS

2	jalapeño peppers	¾	teaspoon garlic salt
1	cup fresh flat-leaf parsley leaves	1	(2-pound) boneless sirloin 3¼-inch-thick, trimmed
1	cup fresh cilantro leaves		
¼	cup water	2	large red onions, thickly sliced
	Juice of 1 lime		
2	teaspoons olive oil	6	poblano peppers (2 pounds), cut into 2-inch-thick strips
2	teaspoons fresh oregano or 1 teaspoon dried		

1 To make the chimichurri sauce, seed 1 of the jalapeños; chop both jalapeños. Put the jalapeños, parsley, cilantro, water, lime juice, oil, oregano, and garlic salt in a mini–food processor and pulse until finely chopped. Transfer ¾ cup of the sauce to a small bowl; cover and refrigerate. Transfer the remaining ¼ cup of sauce to a zip-close plastic bag; add the steak. Squeeze out the air and seal the bag; turn to coat the steak. Refrigerate, turning the bag occasionally, at least 1 hour or overnight.

2 Spray the grill rack with nonstick spray and prepare a medium hot fire. Place the steak on the grill rack and grill until an instant-read thermometer inserted into the side of the steak registers 145°F for medium, 8–9 minutes on each side. Transfer the steak to a cutting board and cover loosely with foil. Let stand 5 minutes.

3 Meanwhile, grill the onions and poblanos until crisp-tender, 5 minutes on each side.

4 Cut the steak crosswise in half. Transfer half of the vegetables (1⅓ cups) and half of the steak to a microwavable bowl and let cool. Cover and refrigerate with ¼ cup of the chimichurri sauce up to 3 days for later use in Speedy Beef Fajitas, opposite. Cut the remaining half of the steak across the grain into 12 slices. Serve with the remaining 1⅓ cups of vegetables and ½ cup of chimichurri sauce.

PER SERVING (3 slices steak with ⅓ cup vegetables and 2 tablespoons sauce): 212 Cal, 6 g Fat, 2 g Sat Fat, 0 g Trans Fat, 73 mg Chol, 138 mg Sod, 9 g Carb, 3 g Fib, 31 g Prot, 37 mg Calc. **POINTS** value: **4.**

...then this! Speedy Beef Fajitas

prep 10 MIN • microwave 3 MIN • serves 4

- ¼   cup reserved chimichurri sauce, 1 pound reserved cooked steak and 1⅓ cups reserved cooked vegetables from Chimichurri Pepper Steak (opposite)
- 3   tablespoons low-fat sour cream
- 4   (8-inch) whole-wheat or multigrain tortillas

1 To make the sauce, mix the chimichurri sauce and sour cream in a small bowl.

2 Transfer the steak from the bowl to a cutting board. Cover the vegetables in the bowl with plastic wrap, prick a few holes in the plastic, and microwave on High just until heated through, 2 minutes, stirring once halfway through.

3 Meanwhile, thinly slice the steak. Microwave the tortillas according to package directions until hot. Divide the steak and vegetables among the tortillas and fold or roll up. Serve with the sauce.

PER SERVING (1 fajita with 1¼ tablespoons sauce): 342 Cal, 9 g Fat, 3 g Sat Fat, 0 g Trans Fat, 83 mg Chol, 357 mg Sod, 31 g Carb, 6 g Fib, 36 g Prot, 85 mg Calc. *POINTS* value: *7.*

make this... Pressure-Cooker Corned Beef

prep 20 MIN • cook 1 HR 5 MIN • serves 4 PLUS LEFTOVERS

1 (3-pound) low-sodium corned beef, trimmed	¾ pound rutabaga, peeled and cut into 1-inch chunks
1 large onion, quartered through the root end	1 pound carrots, peeled and cut into 1-inch chunks
2 teaspoons pickling spice	1 (2-pound) head green cabbage, cut into 6 wedges
1½ pounds Yukon Gold potatoes, peeled and halved	¼ cup whole-grain mustard

1 Place the beef, onion, pickling spice, and enough cold water to cover in a 6-quart pressure cooker. Cover and bring up to high pressure according to the manufacturers' instructions. Reduce the heat to maintain a gentle, steady release of the pressure. Cook until the beef is fork-tender, 1 hour, adjusting the heat as necessary to maintain constant pressure.

2 Remove the cooker from the heat and reduce the pressure quickly according to the manufacturers' instructions. With tongs or a slotted spoon, transfer the beef to a cutting board and cover loosely with foil.

3 Place the potatoes, rutabaga, carrots, and cabbage in the cooking liquid. Return the cooker to the heat and bring to high pressure. Reduce the heat to maintain a gentle, steady release of the pressure. Cook until the vegetables are tender, 5 minutes. Remove the cooker from the heat and reduce the pressure quickly.

4 Discard the cooking liquid. Cut the beef crosswise in half. Transfer half of the vegetables (6 cups) and half of the beef to a container and let cool. Cover and refrigerate up to 4 days for later use in Corned Beef Hash, opposite. Cut the remaining half of beef across the grain into 12 slices. Serve with the remaining vegetables and the mustard.

PER SERVING (3 slices beef with 1½ cups vegetables and 1 tablespoon mustard): 279 Cal, 6 g Fat, 2 g Sat Fat, 0 g Trans Fat, 57 mg Chol, 1,130 mg Sod, 30 g Carb, 6 g Fib, 26 g Prot, 100 mg Calc. **POINTS** value: **5.**

Corned Beef Hash

prep 10 MIN · cook 10 MIN · serves 4

1½ pounds reserved cooked corned beef and 6 cups reserved cooked vegetables from Pressure-Cooker Corned Beef (opposite)

4 scallions, thinly sliced

2 tablespoons spicy brown mustard

¼ teaspoon black pepper

2 teaspoons olive oil

1 Coarsely chop the beef and vegetables; transfer to a large bowl. Stir in the scallions, mustard, and pepper.

2 Heat the oil in a large nonstick skillet over medium-high heat. Add the vegetable mixture and spread evenly to cover the bottom of the skillet with a spatula. Cook, turning occasionally, until heated through and vegetables are golden, about 8 minutes.

PER SERVING (1½ cups): 307 Cal, 8 g Fat, 2 g Sat Fat, 0 g Trans Fat, 57 mg Chol, 1,058 mg Sod, 33 g Carb, 7 g Fib, 27 g Prot, 110 mg Calc. **POINTS** value: **6.**

In the Kitchen

If you don't have pickling spice on hand, you can make your own spice mix for Pressure-Cooker Corned Beef. Instead of the pickling spice, use ¼ teaspoon whole mustard seeds, ¼ teaspoon whole black peppercorns, ¼ teaspoon whole allspice, 1 cinnamon stick, and 1 crumbled bay leaf.

prep 20 MIN • bake/cook 15 MIN • serves 4 PLUS LEFTOVERS

8	taco shells	1	tablespoon chipotle chile powder
2	pounds lean ground beef (5% fat or less)	1	teaspoon dried oregano
1	large onion, chopped	½	teaspoon salt
1	(15-ounce) can tomato sauce	1	cup shredded iceberg lettuce
½	cup ketchup	1	large tomato, diced
1	large green bell pepper, chopped	3	scallions, sliced
1	tablespoon mild cayenne pepper sauce	½	cup fat-free sour cream

1 Preheat the oven to 375°F. Place the taco shells on a baking sheet. Bake until warm, 8 minutes; keep warm.

2 Meanwhile, set a large nonstick skillet over medium-high heat. Add the beef and onion and cook, breaking the beef apart with a wooden spoon, until the beef is browned, about 5 minutes. Drain off any fat then stir in the tomato sauce, ketchup, bell pepper, pepper sauce, chile powder, oregano, and salt. Reduce the heat and cook until thickened and the flavors are blended, 8 minutes.

3 Transfer 1½ cups of the beef mixture to a container and cool. Cover and refrigerate up to 4 days for later use in Beef and Bean Sloppy Joes, opposite. Spoon about ⅓ cup of the remaining beef mixture into each taco shell. Top each evenly with the lettuce, tomato, scallions, and 1 tablespoon of the sour cream.

PER SERVING (2 tacos): 352 Cal, 13 g Fat, 4 g Sat Fat, 2 g Trans Fat, 67 mg Chol, 845 mg Sod, 34 g Carb, 4 g Fib, 27 g Prot, 107 mg Calc. **POINTS** value: **7.**

Beef and Bean Sloppy Joes

prep 10 MIN · cook 10 MIN · serves 6

1½ cups reserved cooked beef mixture from Smoky Beef Tacos (opposite)

1 (15-ounce) can pink or pinto beans, rinsed and drained

¾ cup barbecue sauce

4 scallions, sliced

1½ teaspoons Worcestershire sauce

6 multigrain hamburger buns, split

1 Bring the beef, beans, barbecue sauce, scallions, and Worcestershire sauce just to a boil in a medium saucepan. Reduce the heat and cook, stirring occasionally, until heated through, 5 minutes.

2 Spoon a generous ¾ cup of the filling into each bun.

PER SERVING (1 sloppy Joe): 350 Cal, 6 g Fat, 2 g Sat Fat, 0 g Trans Fat, 43 mg Chol, 1,006 mg Sod, 50 g Carb, 7 g Fib, 24 g Prot, 117 mg Calc. **POINTS** value: **7.**

◆ Filling Extra

For some cheesy kick, sprinkle the filling of each of the Smoky Beef Tacos or the Beef and Bean Sloppy Joes with 1 tablespoon shredded fat-free cheddar cheese.

prep 15 MIN • grill 5 MIN • serves 4 PLUS LEFTOVERS

⅓   cup ketchup

2   teaspoons + 3 tablespoons hoisin sauce

2   pounds lean ground beef (5% fat or less)

⅓   cup chopped fresh cilantro

1½ tablespoons finely chopped peeled fresh ginger

4   scallions, chopped

2   garlic cloves, finely chopped

4   whole-wheat hamburger buns

1 Spray the grill rack with nonstick spray and prepare a medium hot fire.

2 To make the sauce, mix the ketchup and 2 teaspoons of the hoisin sauce in a medium bowl.

3 Gently toss the beef, the remaining 3 tablespoons hoisin sauce, the cilantro, ginger, scallions, and garlic in a large bowl just until blended. Form into 8 patties. Place the burgers on the grill rack and grill, until an instant-read thermometer inserted into the side of each burger registers 160°F for medium, 3–4 minutes on each side. Wrap and refrigerate 4 of the burgers up to 3 days for later use in Korean Beef in Lettuce Cups, opposite. Top the remaining 4 burgers evenly with the sauce and serve in the buns.

PER SERVING (1 burger with generous 1 tablespoon sauce): 306 Cal, 9 g Fat, 3 g Sat Fat, 1 g Trans Fat, 64 mg Chol, 614 mg Sod, 28 g Carb, 3 g Fib, 29 g Prot, 68 mg Calc. **POINTS** value: **6.**

Korean Beef in Lettuce Cups

prep 15 MIN • microwave 5 MIN • serves 4

4 **reserved cooked burgers from Hoisin Burgers (opposite), chopped**	**¼ cup chopped fresh mint**
1 cup chopped red bell pepper	**Juice of 1 lime**
4 scallions, thinly sliced	**¼ teaspoon hot pepper sauce**
1 cup shredded carrots	**8 Boston lettuce leaves**

1 Place the burgers in a 1½-quart microwavable dish and sprinkle with the bell pepper. Cover with plastic wrap; then prick a few holes in the plastic. Microwave on High until heated through, 3 minutes. Stir in the scallions, carrots, mint, lime juice, and pepper sauce.

2 Place the lettuce leaves on a platter. Fill each leaf with ½ cup of the beef mixture.

PER SERVING (2 lettuce leaves with 1 cup beef mixture): 206 Cal, 7 g Fat, 3 g Sat Fat, 0 g Trans Fat, 64 mg Chol, 176 mg Sod, 11 g Carb, 3 g Fib, 24 g Prot, 51 mg Calc. **POINTS** value: **4.**

◆ Filling Extra

For a heartier meal, skip the lettuce and spoon 1 cup of the beef mixture over ½ cup cooked brown rice and increase the **POINTS** value by **2.**

make this... Old-Fashioned Meatloaf

prep 20 MIN · cook 1 HR 5 MIN · serves 4 PLUS LEFTOVERS

1 **large carrot, cut into 1-inch chunks**	½ **cup plain dried bread crumbs**
1 **zucchini, cut into 1-inch chunks**	2 **large eggs**
5 **scallions, cut into 1-inch pieces**	1 **teaspoon dried Italian seasoning**
2¼ **pounds lean meatloaf mix (beef, pork, and veal)**	1 **teaspoon salt**
	½ **teaspoon black pepper**
½ **cup low-fat milk**	½ **cup finely chopped roasted red bell pepper**

1 Preheat the oven to 375°F.

2 Put the carrots in a food processor and pulse until finely chopped. Add the zucchini and scallions; pulse until chopped. Spray a large nonstick skillet with nonstick spray and set over medium heat. Add the vegetables and cook, stirring occasionally, until softened, 6 minutes. Transfer to a large bowl and let cool, 10 minutes. Stir in the remaining ingredients just until blended.

3 Divide the mixture in half. Form into 2 (4 x 7-inch) loaves and place 2 inches apart in a 9 x 13-inch baking dish. Bake until an instant-read thermometer inserted into the center of each loaf registers 160°F, 1 hour. Transfer to a cutting board and let stand 10 minutes.

4 Let 1 of the meatloaves cool. Wrap and refrigerate up to 4 days for later use in Italian Wedding Soup, opposite. Cut the remaining meatloaf into 8 slices and top each serving with 2 tablespoons of the roasted bell pepper.

PER SERVING (2 slices): 305 Cal, 12 g Fat, 5 g Sat Fat, 0 g Trans Fat, 157 mg Chol, 1,178 mg Sod, 23 g Carb, 2 g Fib, 26 g Prot, 146 mg Calc. *POINTS* value: *7.*

Italian Wedding Soup

prep 10 MIN · cook 10 min · serves 6

2   (14½-ounce) cans low-sodium chicken broth

2   cups water

1   (16-ounce) package frozen mixed Italian vegetables

1   teaspoon dried Italian seasoning

1   reserved cooked meatloaf from Old-Fashioned Meatloaf (opposite), cut into ½-inch chunks

⅓   cup chopped fresh parsley

¼   cup grated Parmesan cheese

Bring the broth and water to a boil in a large saucepan. Stir in the mixed vegetables and Italian seasoning; return to a boil. Reduce the heat and cook, stirring occasionally, until the vegetables are heated through, 5 minutes. Add the meatloaf and parsley; cook until heated through, 2 minutes. Serve with the cheese.

PER SERVING (generous 1 cup soup with 2 teaspoons cheese): 265 Cal, 10 g Fat, 4 g Sat Fat, 0 g Trans Fat, 108 mg Chol, 922 mg Sod, 21 g Carb, 3 g Fib, 24 g Prot, 188 mg Calc. *POINTS* value: *6.*

Beef in Tomato-Ginger Sauce

prep 20 MIN · cook 30 MIN · serves 4 PLUS LEFTOVERS

1¾ pounds lean ground beef or lamb (5% fat or less)	2 tablespoons red-wine vinegar
1 teaspoon olive oil	2 tablespoons finely chopped peeled fresh ginger
2 large yellow bell peppers, coarsely chopped	4 teaspoons smoked paprika
1 large red onion, coarsely chopped	2 teaspoons ground cumin
1 (14½-ounce) can diced tomatoes	1¼ teaspoons salt
¼ cup water	1 (8-ounce) can tomato sauce
2 tablespoons tomato paste	1½ cups frozen peas
2 tablespoons honey	

1 Set a large nonstick skillet over medium-high heat. Add the beef and brown, breaking it apart with a wooden spoon. Drain off any fat then transfer to a medium bowl.

2 Heat the oil in the skillet over medium heat. Add the bell peppers and onion; cook, stirring occasionally, until crisp-tender, 8 minutes. Add the beef, tomatoes, water, tomato paste, honey, vinegar, ginger, paprika, cumin, and salt; bring just to a boil. Reduce the heat and cook, stirring occasionally, until the vegetables are tender and the flavors are blended, 8 minutes.

3 Transfer 2 cups of the beef mixture to a container and let cool. Cover and refrigerate up to 4 days for later use in Lebanese Pita Pizzas, opposite. Add the tomato sauce and peas to the remaining beef mixture; cook until the peas are tender, 5 minutes.

PER SERVING (1½ cups): 349 Cal, 11 g Fat, 4 g Sat Fat, 0 g Trans Fat, 84 mg Chol, 1,117 mg Sod, 30 g Carb, 6 g Fib, 35 g Prot, 83 mg Calc. *POINTS* value: *7.*

Lebanese Pita Pizzas

prep 10 MIN · bake 10 MIN · serves 4

2   cups reserved cooked beef mixture from Beef in Tomato-Ginger Sauce (opposite)

3   tablespoons chopped fresh mint

¼   teaspoon cinnamon

2   (6-inch) whole-wheat pitas, split

2   tablespoons chopped pitted kalamata olives

1   cup crumbled low-fat feta cheese

1 Preheat the oven to 450°F.

2 Mix the beef mixture, mint, and cinnamon in a medium bowl.

3 Place the pitas, cut side up, on a baking sheet. Spread ½ cup of the beef mixture onto each pita half. Sprinkle evenly with the olives and cheese. Bake until heated through, 8 minutes.

PER SERVING (1 pizza): 247 Cal, 8 g Fat, 3 g Sat Fat, 0 g Trans Fat, 40 mg Chol, 873 mg Sod, 28 g Carb, 3 g Fib, 19 g Prot, 172 mg Calc. **POINTS** value: **5.**

prep 15 MIN • roast 1 HR 15 MIN • serves 4 PLUS LEFTOVERS

1¼ pounds sweet potatoes, peeled and cut into
    ¾-inch chunks

1   large sweet onion, cut into thin wedges

½   cup water

½   cup Asian sweet chili-garlic sauce

1   tablespoon ancho chile powder

2   teaspoons grated peeled fresh ginger

1   (2-pound) boneless pork loin, trimmed

1 Preheat the oven to 450°F. Mix the potatoes, onion, and water in a 9 x 13-inch baking dish; bake 15 minutes.

2 Meanwhile, mix the chili-garlic sauce, chile powder, and ginger in a small bowl.

3 Remove the baking dish from the oven; place the pork in the center of the dish on top of the vegetables. Brush the pork and the vegetables with ¼ cup of the chili mixture. Bake 10 minutes. Reduce the oven temperature to 300°F and bake 35 minutes. Brush the pork and vegetables with the remaining chili mixture and bake until the potatoes are fork-tender and an instant-read thermometer inserted into the center of the pork registers 160°F, 15 minutes. Transfer the pork to a cutting board; cover the pork and vegetables loosely with foil. Let stand 10 minutes.

4 Cut the pork crosswise in half. Let half of the pork cool. Wrap and refrigerate up to 3 days for later use in Pork and Bok Choy Noodle Bowl, opposite. Cut the remaining half of pork into 8 slices and serve with the vegetables.

PER SERVING (2 slices pork with ¾ cup vegetables): 272 Cal, 5 g Fat, 2 g Sat Fat, 0 g Trans Fat, 72 mg Chol, 432 mg Sod, 27 g Carb, 5 g Fib, 28 g Prot, 55 mg Calc. *POINTS* value: *5.*

Pork and Bok Choy Noodle Bowl

prep 15 MIN · cook 20 MIN · serves 4

¼ pound whole-wheat spaghetti

1 (32-ounce) carton low-sodium chicken broth

2 tablespoons low-sodium soy sauce

2 tablespoons Asian sweet chili-garlic sauce

1 tablespoon grated peeled fresh ginger

1 pound baby bok choy, quartered

1½ cups shredded carrots

1 pound reserved cooked pork from Double Chili Pork Roast (opposite), thinly sliced

1 Cook the spaghetti according to the package directions, omitting the salt if desired. Drain, reserving 2 cups of the cooking liquid.

2 Mix the broth, the reserved cooking liquid, soy sauce, chili-garlic sauce, and ginger in the pasta pot; bring to a boil. Add the bok choy and carrots; reduce the heat and simmer, stirring occasionally, until the vegetables are tender, 5 minutes. Add the spaghetti and pork; cook, stirring occasionally, until heated through, 2 minutes.

PER SERVING (about 2¼ cups): 351 Cal, 7 g Fat, 2 g Sat Fat, 0 g Trans Fat, 72 mg Chol, 952 mg Sod, 38 g Carb, 6 g Fib, 37 g Prot, 162 mg Calc. POINTS value: 7.

In the Kitchen

If baby bok choy isn't available at your supermarket, substitute 1 pound Swiss chard or collard greens, trimmed and cut into 1-inch slices.

make this... Chipotle Roast Pork

prep 20 MIN • roast 45 MIN • serves 4 PLUS LEFTOVERS

2	(1-pound) pork tenderloins, trimmed
2	tablespoons barbecue sauce or salsa
1	seeded and finely chopped chipotle en adobo + 4 teaspoons adobo sauce
2	teaspoons ground cumin

	Grated zest of 1 small lime
1	large red onion, quartered and sliced
1½	pounds zucchini, cut lengthwise in half and sliced
3	large red bell peppers, thinly sliced
½	teaspoon salt

1 Place an oven rack on the upper and lower rungs of the oven; preheat the oven to 475°F. Spray a large heavy rimmed baking pan with nonstick spray.

2 Spray a 9 x 13-inch baking dish with nonstick spray; place the pork in the dish. Mix the barbecue sauce, chipotle en adobo, 2 teaspoons of the adobo sauce, the cumin, and lime zest in a small bowl; brush evenly over the pork. Place the onion around the pork. Toss the zucchini, bell peppers, and salt on the prepared baking pan.

3 Place the pork on the upper rack and the vegetables on the lower rack in the oven. Roast the pork until an instant-read thermometer inserted into the center of each tenderloin registers 160°F, 35 minutes. Transfer to a cutting board and cover loosely with foil; reserve the onion and pan drippings. Roast the vegetables until browned and tender, 10 minutes longer.

4 Toss the vegetables, the reserved onion and pan drippings, and the remaining 2 teaspoons of adobo sauce in a large bowl until blended. Transfer half of the vegetables (4 cups) and 1 of the tenderloins to a container and let cool. Cover and refrigerate up to 3 days for later use in Mexican Pork and Veggie Bake, opposite. Cut the remaining tenderloin into 8 slices and serve with the remaining 4 cups of vegetables.

PER SERVING (2 slices pork with 1 cup vegetables): 210 Cal, 5 g Fat, 2 g Sat Fat, 0 g Trans Fat, 72 mg Chol, 387 mg Sod, 14 g Carb, 4 g Fib, 28 g Prot, 42 mg Calc. **POINTS** value: **4.**

...then this! ## Mexican Pork and Veggie Bake

prep 20 MIN • cook/bake 1 HR • serves 4

1	pound sweet potatoes, peeled and thinly sliced	1	cup enchilada sauce
1	reserved cooked pork tenderloin and 4 cups reserved cooked vegetables from Chipotle Roast Pork (opposite)	⅓	cup chopped fresh cilantro
		1	tablespoon plain dried bread crumbs
1	cup frozen corn kernels	1½	teaspoons chili powder
		¼	teaspoon salt

1 Preheat the oven to 425°F. Spray an 8-inch square baking dish with nonstick spray.

2 Meanwhile, bring a large saucepan of lightly salted water to a boil. Add the potatoes and cook until just tender, 8 minutes. Drain and let cool.

3 Dice the pork and transfer to a large bowl. Stir in the vegetables, corn, ¾ cup of the enchilada sauce, the cilantro, bread crumbs, chili powder, and salt.

4 Spread half of the potatoes in the bottom of the prepared baking dish. Top evenly with the pork mixture and the remaining potatoes and ¼ cup of enchilada sauce. Cover with foil and bake until hot in the center, 45 minutes.

PER SERVING (2¼ cups): 312 Cal, 6 g Fat, 2 g Sat Fat, 0 g Trans Fat, 72 mg Chol, 920 mg Sod, 37 g Carb, 7 g Fib, 31 g Prot, 77 mg Calc. **POINTS** value: **6.**

◆ Filling Extra

A citrus-jicama salad is a perfect accompaniment to either the Chipotle Roast Pork or the Mexican Pork and Veggie Bake. Mix 2 peeled and sectioned navel oranges, 2 cups matchstick-thin strips jicama, 1 thinly sliced red bell pepper, and salt and black pepper to taste.

make this... Salsa Verde Pork Stew

prep 35 MIN • cook 1 HR • serves 4 PLUS LEFTOVERS

2   pounds boneless pork loin, trimmed and cut into ¾-inch chunks

2   large onions, coarsely chopped

1   (14½-ounce) can low-sodium chicken broth

4   garlic cloves, coarsely chopped

1½ teaspoons ground cumin

1   teaspoon dried oregano

¼   cup water

2   tablespoons all-purpose flour

3   zucchini, quartered lengthwise and sliced

1   (15-ounce) can white beans, rinsed and drained

1   cup fat-free salsa verde

1 Spray a large nonstick Dutch oven with nonstick spray and set over medium-high heat. Add the pork, in batches if necessary, and cook, turning occasionally, until browned, about 6 minutes. Transfer with a slotted spoon to a medium bowl. Add the onions to the Dutch oven and cook, stirring occasionally, until golden, about 5 minutes. Add the broth, garlic, cumin, and oregano; bring to a boil, scraping up the browned bits from the bottom of the Dutch oven. Stir in the pork and reduce the heat. Cover and simmer 30 minutes.

2 Meanwhile, whisk the water and flour in a small bowl until blended. Add the flour mixture, zucchini, beans, and salsa to the Dutch oven, stirring until blended. Simmer uncovered until the pork and zucchini are tender, 8 minutes.

3 Transfer 2½ cups of the stew to a small microwavable bowl and let cool. Cover and refrigerate up to 4 days for later use in Pork Tostadas, opposite. Divide the remaining 5 cups of stew among 4 bowls.

PER SERVING (1¼ cups stew): 338 Cal, 10 g Fat, 3 g Sat Fat, 0 g Trans Fat, 72 mg Chol, 366 mg Sod, 29 g Carb, 7 g Fib, 35 g Prot, 104 mg Calc. **POINTS** value: **7.**

...then this! Pork Tostadas

prep 10 MIN · bake/microwave 5 MIN · serves 4

4	**(6-inch) multigrain tortillas**
2½	**cups reserved cooked Salsa Verde Pork Stew (opposite)**
2	**cups shredded romaine lettuce**
1	**tomato, diced**
¼	**cup chopped fresh cilantro**
¼	**cup fat-free sour cream**

1 Preheat the oven to 400°F. Lightly spray both sides of the tortillas with nonstick spray and place on a baking sheet. Bake until crisp around the edges, 6 minutes.

2 Meanwhile, break up the chunks of the pork from the stew with a large spoon. Cover with plastic wrap; then prick a few holes in the plastic. Microwave on High until heated through, 3 minutes.

3 Spoon ⅔ cup of the stew onto each tortilla. Top each with ½ cup of the lettuce, one-fourth of the tomato, and 1 tablespoon each cilantro and sour cream.

PER SERVING (1 tostada):
284 Cal, 9 g Fat, 3 g Sat Fat,
0 g Trans Fat, 50 mg Chol,
321 mg Sod, 29 g Carb,
6 g Fib, 25 g Prot,
86 mg Calc.
POINTS value: **6.**

Orange-Glazed Pork Chops with Fennel

prep 20 MIN • bake 45 MIN • serves 4 PLUS LEFTOVERS

6 carrots, cut into matchstick-thin strips	½ teaspoon salt
2 red onions, each cut into 8 wedges through the root end	¼ teaspoon black pepper
	3 tablespoons honey Dijon mustard
1 large fennel bulb, cut into ¼-inch wedges through the root end	3 tablespoons all-fruit orange marmalade
	7 (5-ounce) bone-in pork loin chops, trimmed
2 teaspoons olive oil	1 tablespoon white balsamic vinegar
1½ teaspoons fennel seeds, crushed	

1 Place an oven rack on the upper and lower rungs of the oven; preheat the oven to 425°F.

2 Mix the carrots, onions, and fennel on a large heavy rimmed baking pan. Drizzle with the oil and sprinkle with 1 teaspoon of the fennel seeds, the salt, and pepper; toss well. Spread the vegetables evenly in the pan; cover the pan with foil. Place the pan on the lower rack in the oven and bake 25 minutes. Uncover and bake just until tender, 20 minutes.

3 Meanwhile, mix the mustard, marmalade, and the remaining ½ teaspoon of fennel seeds in a small bowl. Spray another heavy rimmed baking pan with nonstick spray. Place the pork on the prepared baking pan and spread the mustard mixture evenly over each chop.

4 About 15 minutes before the cooking time for the vegetables is up, place the pork on the upper rack in the oven and bake until an instant-read thermometer inserted into the side of each chop registers 160°F, 15 minutes. Toss the vegetables with the vinegar.

5 Transfer 2 cups of the vegetables and 3 of the chops to a container and let cool. Cover and refrigerate up to 3 days for later use in Lemony Pork and Lentil Salad, opposite. Serve the remaining 4 chops with the remaining 4 cups of vegetables.

PER SERVING (1 pork chop with 1 cup vegetables): 271 Cal, 10 g Fat, 3 g Sat Fat, 0 g Trans Fat, 64 mg Chol, 360 mg Sod, 21 g Carb, 5 g Fib, 24 g Prot, 67 mg Calc. **POINTS** value: **5.**

Lemony Pork and Lentil Salad

prep 15 MIN • cook NONE • serves 4

3	reserved cooked pork chops and 2 cups reserved cooked vegetables from Orange-Glazed Pork Chops with Fennel (opposite)
	Grated zest and juice of 1 small lemon
1	tablespoon honey Dijon mustard
2	teaspoons olive oil

1	teaspoon honey
½	teaspoon salt
1	(15-ounce) can lentils, rinsed and drained
2	scallions, sliced
2	tomatoes, diced
1	cup chopped celery

1 Dice the pork and vegetables.

2 Whisk the lemon zest and juice, mustard, oil, honey, and salt in a large bowl. Add the pork, vegetables, lentils, scallions, tomatoes, and celery; toss to coat.

PER SERVING (1¾ cups): 325 Cal, 10 g Fat, 3 g Sat Fat, 0 g Trans Fat, 48 mg Chol, 732 mg Sod, 35 g Carb, 8 g Fib, 25 g Prot, 76 mg Calc. **POINTS** value: **7.**

◆ Filling Extra

Top each serving with 2 tablespoons plain fat-free yogurt and 1 tablespoon chopped fresh cilantro.

make this... Miso-Glazed Pork

prep 20 MIN • **cook** 45 MIN • **serves** 4 PLUS LEFTOVERS

- **3** tablespoons rice vinegar
- **3** tablespoons packed brown sugar
- **3** tablespoons light miso
- **2** teaspoons grated peeled fresh ginger
- **7** (¼-pound) boneless pork loin chops, trimmed

- **1** tablespoon chopped fresh cilantro
- **1½** pounds carrots, sliced
- **12** shallots, halved lengthwise

1 Mix 2 tablespoons of the vinegar, 2 tablespoons of the brown sugar, the miso, and ginger in a medium bowl. Transfer ¼ cup of the miso mixture to a zip-close plastic bag; add the pork. Squeeze out the air and seal the bag; turn to coat the pork. Refrigerate, turning the bag occasionally, at least 1 hour or overnight. To make the sauce, stir the cilantro and the remaining 1 tablespoon of vinegar and 1 tablespoon of brown sugar into the remaining miso mixture; cover and refrigerate.

2 Preheat the oven to 450°F. Line a rimmed baking pan with foil. Spread the carrots in a single layer over three quarters of the pan and the shallots over the remaining pan. Cover the pan with foil and bake 20 minutes.

3 Remove the pan from the oven. Reduce the oven temperature to 300°F. Push the carrots and shallots toward the sides of the pan. Place the chops in a single layer in the center of the pan. Bake uncovered until an instant-read thermometer inserted into the center of each chop registers 160°F, 25 minutes.

4 Transfer ¾ cup of the carrots and 3 of the chops to a container and let cool. Cover and refrigerate up to 3 days for later use in Pork Fried Rice, opposite. Serve the remaining 4 chops and 2 cups of carrots with the shallots and the sauce.

PER SERVING (1 pork chop with about ¾ cup vegetables and 4 teaspoons sauce): 307 Cal, 9 g Fat, 3 g Sat Fat, 0 g Trans Fat, 70 mg Chol, 420 mg Sod, 28 g Carb, 4 g Fib, 28 g Prot, 68 mg Calc. ***POINTS*** value: **6.**

Pork Fried Rice

prep 10 MIN · cook 5 MIN · serves 4

3 reserved cooked pork chops and ¾ cup reserved cooked carrots from Miso-Glazed Pork (opposite)

2 teaspoons canola oil

5 scallions, sliced

1 cup frozen peas

2 teaspoons grated peeled fresh ginger

3 (125-gram) cartons cooked brown rice (about 3 cups)

⅓ cup fat-free stir-fry sauce

1 Dice the pork.

2 Heat a large skillet over high heat until a drop of water sizzles on it. Pour in the oil and swirl to coat the skillet; then add the scallions. Stir-fry until softened, 1 minute.

3 Add the carrots, peas, and ginger; stir fry until the peas are hot, 1 minute. Add the pork, rice, and stir-fry sauce; cook, stirring frequently, until heated through, 3 minutes.

PER SERVING (1½ cups): 357 Cal, 10 g Fat, 3 g Sat Fat, 0 g Trans Fat, 52 mg Chol, 720 mg Sod, 42 g Carb, 6 g Fib, 24 g Prot, 49 mg Calc. **POINTS** value: **7.**

Balsamic Sausage and Peppers

prep 20 MIN • bake/cook 20 MIN • serves 6 PLUS LEFTOVERS

8   Italian sausage links (1½ pounds), pierced with a fork

4   assorted-color bell peppers, thinly sliced

2   sweet onions, sliced

3   zucchini, cut into ¼-inch-thick matchstick strips

3   large garlic cloves, thinly sliced

1   teaspoon fennel seeds, crushed

½   teaspoon salt

2   tablespoons balsamic vinegar

1   teaspoon honey

¼   cup thinly sliced fresh basil

1 Preheat the oven to 475°F.

2 Place the sausages a 1½-quart shallow baking dish and bake until cooked through, 15 minutes. Transfer the sausages to a cutting board and let stand 5 minutes.

3 Meanwhile, spray a 12-inch nonstick skillet with nonstick spray and set over medium-high heat. Add the bell peppers and onions; cook, stirring occasionally, until crisp-tender, 12 minutes. Add the zucchini, garlic, fennel seeds, and salt; cook, stirring occasionally, until the vegetables are just tender, 6 minutes. Stir in the vinegar and honey.

4 Transfer 2 cups of the vegetables and 4 of the sausages to a container and let cool. Cover and refrigerate up to 3 days for later use in Sausage Shepherd's Pie, opposite. Slice the remaining 4 sausages. Transfer to a large bowl, stir in the remaining 4 cups of vegetables, and sprinkle with the basil.

PER SERVING (generous 1 cup): 189 Cal, 12 g Fat, 4 g Sat Fat, 0 g Trans Fat, 24 mg Chol, 639 mg Sod, 12 g Carb, 2 g Fib, 10 g Prot, 40 mg Calc. **POINTS** value: **4.**

Sausage Shepherd's Pie

prep 20 MIN · cook 30 MIN · serves 6

1¼ pounds all-purpose potatoes, peeled and cut into 1-inch chunks

3 tablespoons grated Parmesan cheese

½ teaspoon salt

4 reserved cooked sausages and 2 cups reserved cooked vegetables from Balsamic Sausage and Peppers (opposite)

1 (14½-ounce) can Italian-style diced tomatoes, drained

1 Bring the potatoes and enough water to cover to a boil in a large saucepan. Reduce the heat and cook until fork-tender, 15 minutes. Drain, reserving ⅔ cup of the cooking liquid. Return the potatoes to the pan. Add the reserved cooking liquid, cheese, and salt; mash until blended.

2 Meanwhile, dice the sausages and coarsely chop the vegetables. Mix the sausages, vegetables, and tomatoes in a medium skillet. Bring to a boil. Reduce the heat and cook until slightly thickened, 6 minutes.

3 Spoon the mashed potatoes evenly over the sausage mixture, leaving a 1-inch border. Cover and cook until heated through, 4 minutes.

PER SERVING (1⅓ cups): 262 Cal, 13 g Fat, 5 g Sat Fat, 0 g Trans Fat, 26 mg Chol, 905 mg Sod, 26 g Carb, 3 g Fib, 12 g Prot, 89 mg Calc. *POINTS* value: **6.**

◆ Filling Extra

If you have some fat-free ricotta cheese handy, add 2–3 tablespoons when mashing the potatoes in step 1.

Ham with Fresh Peach Chutney

prep 20 MIN • cook 15 MIN • serves 4 PLUS LEFTOVERS

1 teaspoon olive oil	2 teaspoons grated peeled fresh ginger
1 small red bell pepper, chopped	1 tablespoon red-wine vinegar
3 small peaches, cut into wedges	2 teaspoons honey
2 scallions, sliced	4 (6-ounce) low-sodium boneless ham steaks
3 tablespoons chutney, chopped	

1 To make the chutney, heat the oil in a large nonstick skillet over medium heat. Add the bell pepper and cook, stirring occasionally, until crisp-tender, 4 minutes. Add the peaches and scallions; cook, stirring occasionally, just until the peaches soften, 2 minutes. Add the chutney, ginger, vinegar, and honey; cook until the flavors are blended, 1 minute. Transfer to a bowl.

2 Add the ham to the skillet and cook until browned and heated through, about 3 minutes on each side.

3 Let 2 of the ham steaks cool. Wrap and refrigerate up to 3 days for later use in Ham and Apple Slaw, opposite. Cut the remaining 2 ham steaks in half and serve with the chutney.

PER SERVING (½ ham steak with ½ cup chutney): 194 Cal, 6 g Fat, 2 g Sat Fat, 0 g Trans Fat, 40 mg Chol, 744 mg Sod, 19 g Carb, 2 g Fib, 17 g Prot, 21 mg Calc. ***POINTS*** value: *4.*

Ham and Apple Slaw

prep 10 MIN • cook NONE • serves 4

2 reserved cooked ham steaks from Ham with Fresh Peach Chutney, cut into matchstick-thin strips

1 (16-ounce) package coleslaw mix

1 apple, diced

1 cup shredded carrots

⅓ cup low-fat Asian sesame dressing

1 tablespoon red-wine vinegar

1 tablespoon chopped smoked almonds

Mix the ham, coleslaw mix, apple, carrots, sesame dressing, and vinegar in a large bowl. Top with the almonds.

PER SERVING (about 2 cups): 195 Cal, 6 g Fat, 2 g Sat Fat, 0 g Trans Fat, 40 mg Chol, 1,017 mg Sod, 17 g Carb, 4 g Fib, 18 g Prot, 68 mg Calc. **POINTS** value: **4.**

make this... Roast Lamb with Bulgur and Mint Pesto

prep 35 MIN • **bake** 1 HR 30 MIN • **serves** 4 PLUS LEFTOVERS

1 cup fresh mint leaves	1 (2-pound) boned leg of lamb, trimmed and tied
1 cup fresh parsley leaves	
¼ cup water	2 teaspoons olive oil
3 garlic cloves	Juice of ¼ lemon
2 teaspoons grated lemon zest	2 teaspoons butter
	3 large shallots, chopped
½ teaspoon salt	1½ cups bulgur
¼ teaspoon black pepper	2⅔ cups low-sodium chicken broth
¾ teaspoon ground coriander	

1 Preheat the oven to 350°F.

2 To make the pesto, puree the mint, parsley, water, garlic, lemon zest, salt, pepper, and ¼ teaspoon of the coriander in a mini–food processor. Transfer ¼ cup of the pesto to a cup and stir in the remaining ½ teaspoon of coriander. Place the lamb in a shallow baking dish; spread with the ¼ cup pesto and coriander mixture. Roast the lamb until an instant-read thermometer inserted into the center registers 160°F for medium, 1 hour 30 minutes. Transfer the lamb to a cutting board and cover loosely with foil. Let stand 15 minutes.

3 Meanwhile, to make the sauce, mix the remaining ½ cup pesto, the oil, and lemon juice in a small bowl.

4 To make the bulgur, melt the butter in a large saucepan over medium-low heat. Add the shallots and cook, stirring occasionally, until softened, 2 minutes. Add the bulgur and cook, stirring occasionally, until toasted and fragrant, about 5 minutes. Stir in the broth and bring just to a boil. Reduce the heat; cover and simmer 5 minutes. Remove the saucepan from the heat. Let the bulgur stand until tender and the liquid is absorbed, 10 minutes.

5 Fluff the bulgur with a fork. Cut the lamb crosswise in half. Transfer half of the bulgur (2 cups) and half of the lamb to a microwavable bowl and let cool. Cover and refrigerate up to 3 days for later use in Lamb Tagine with Apricots, opposite. Cut the remaining half of lamb into 12 slices and serve with the remaining 2 cups of bulgur and the sauce.

PER SERVING (3 slices lamb with ½ cup bulgur and 1½ tablespoons sauce): 314 Cal, 11 g Fat, 4 g Sat Fat, 0 g Trans Fat, 81 mg Chol, 300 mg Sod, 25 g Carb, 6 g Fib, 55 g Prot, 00 mg Calc. **POINTS** value: **6.**

Lamb Tagine with Apricots

prep 15 MIN • cook 15 MIN • serves 6

- **1** **pound reserved cooked lamb and 2 cups reserved cooked bulgur from Roast Lamb with Bulgur Mint Pesto (opposite)**
- **1** **(14½-ounce) can diced tomatoes with sweet onions**
- **1** **cup canned chickpeas, rinsed and drained**
- **¼** **cup all-fruit orange marmalade**
- **6** **dried apricots, sliced**
- **1** **teaspoon curry powder**
- **½** **teaspoon ground cumin**
- **½** **teaspoon chicken or beef bouillon powder**
- **⅛** **teaspoon ground allspice**
- **2** **zucchini, diced**

1 To make the tagine, dice the lamb. Bring the tomatoes, chickpeas, marmalade, apricots, curry powder, cumin, bouillon powder, and allspice just to a boil in a large saucepan. Reduce the heat and cook until slightly thickened, 6 minutes. Stir in the zucchini and cook just until tender, 6 minutes. Stir in the lamb and cook until heated through, 3 minutes.

2 Meanwhile, cover the bulgur with plastic wrap; then prick a few holes in the plastic. Microwave on High until heated through, 1½ minutes. Serve with the tagine.

PER SERVING (1 cup tagine with ⅓ cup bulgur): 321 Cal, 8 g Fat, 3 g Sat Fat, 0 g Trans Fat, 54 mg Chol, 307 mg Sod, 41 g Carb, 8 g Fib, 24 g Prot, 79 mg Calc. **POINTS** value: **6.**

make this... Lamb and Vegetable Stew

prep 30 MIN • cook 1 HR 30 MIN • serves 4 PLUS LEFTOVERS

2   pounds boneless leg of lamb, trimmed and cut into ¾-inch chunks

¼   cup all-purpose flour

2   teaspoons paprika

1   teaspoon salt

½   teaspoon black pepper

3   teaspoons canola oil

2   large onions, chopped

4   garlic cloves, minced

1   (14½-ounce) can low-sodium chicken broth

1   cup dry red wine

2   pounds carrots, cut into 1-inch pieces

2   parsnips, peeled and cut into 1-inch pieces

1   pound green beans, trimmed and halved

2   teaspoons chopped fresh thyme or ½ teaspoon dried

1 Toss the lamb, flour, paprika, salt, and pepper in a medium bowl until evenly coated.

2 Heat 1½ teaspoons of the oil in a Dutch oven over medium-high heat. Add half of the lamb and cook until browned on all sides, about 5 minutes. Transfer to a plate. Repeat with the remaining 1½ teaspoons of oil and half of lamb.

3 Add the onions and garlic to the Dutch oven; cook, scraping up the browned bits from the bottom of the Dutch oven, until softened, 5 minutes. Stir in the lamb, broth, wine, carrots, and parsnips; bring to a boil. Reduce the heat; cover and simmer 1 hour. Stir in the beans. Simmer, covered, until the lamb and vegetables are fork-tender, 15 minutes.

4 Transfer half of the stew (about 5 cups) to a container and let cool. Cover and refrigerate up to 3 days for later use in Lamb-Noodle Casserole, opposite. Stir the thyme into the remaining 5 cups of stew and simmer 2 minutes.

PER SERVING (1¼ cups): 318 Cal, 10 g Fat, 3 g Sat Fat, 0 g Trans Fat, 78 mg Chol, 458 mg Sod, 28 g Carb, 7 g Fib, 28 g Prot, 91 mg Calc. *POINTS* value: **6.**

Lamb-Noodle Casserole

prep 10 MIN • cook/bake 35 MIN • serves 6

¼   **pound whole-grain yolk-free wide noodles**

5   **cups reserved cooked Lamb and Vegetable Stew (opposite)**

1   **(15-ounce) can tomato sauce**

½   **cup shredded fat-free cheddar cheese**

2   **tablespoons seasoned dried bread crumbs**

2   **tablespoons grated Parmesan cheese**

1 Preheat the oven to 350°F. Spray a 2-quart baking dish with nonstick spray.

2 Cook the noodles according to the package directions, omitting the salt if desired.

3 Meanwhile, mix the stew and tomato sauce in a medium saucepan and set over medium heat. Cook, stirring occasionally, until heated through, about 10 minutes.

4 Drain the noodles, stir into the lamb mixture, and spoon into the prepared baking dish. Mix the cheddar, bread crumbs, and Parmesan in a small bowl. Sprinkle evenly over the lamb mixture. Cover the baking dish with nonstick foil and bake 10 minutes. Uncover and bake until heated through and the cheese is melted, 5 minutes.

PER SERVING (generous 1 cup): 353 Cal, 8 g Fat, 3 g Sat Fat, 0 g Trans Fat, 55 mg Chol, 911 mg Sod, 43 g Carb, 7 g Fib, 27 g Prot, 193 mg Calc. **POINTS** value: **7.**

In the Kitchen

If you don't have nonstick foil handy, spray a sheet of regular foil with nonstick spray. That will prevent the cheese from sticking to the foil while the casserole bakes.

Veal Stew Marsala

prep 35 MIN · cook 1 HR 30 MIN · serves 4 PLUS LEFTOVERS

2 pounds veal for stew, cut into 3/4-inch chunks	¾ teaspoon dried thyme
⅓ cup + 1 tablespoon all-purpose flour	½ teaspoon dried tarragon
3 teaspoons olive oil	¼ teaspoon black pepper
1 (14½-ounce) can low-sodium chicken broth	1 pound carrots, halved lengthwise and sliced
1 (14½-ounce) can diced tomatoes	4 parsnips, peeled and diced
¾ cup Marsala or dry white wine	2 leeks, trimmed to white and light green parts, cleaned, and cut into ¾-inch pieces
1 (10-ounce) package fresh mushrooms, halved	
2 garlic cloves, chopped	2 tablespoons water
1¼ teaspoons salt	1 tablespoon white-wine vinegar

1 Toss the veal and ⅓ cup of the flour in a medium bowl until evenly coated. Heat 1½ teaspoons of the oil in a large Dutch oven over medium-high heat. Add half of the veal and cook, turning occasionally, until browned, about 6 minutes. Transfer to a medium bowl with a slotted spoon. Repeat with the remaining 1½ teaspoons of oil and half of veal.

2 Add the broth and cook, scraping up the browned bits from the bottom of the Dutch oven. Stir in the veal, tomatoes, Marsala, mushrooms, garlic, salt, thyme, tarragon, and pepper; bring to a boil. Reduce the heat; cover and simmer 45 minutes. Stir in the carrots, parsnips, and leeks. Cover and simmer until the veal and vegetables are fork-tender, 20 minutes.

3 Meanwhile, whisk the water and the remaining 1 tablespoon of flour in a cup until blended. Add the flour mixture to the stew, stirring constantly, until blended. Simmer, uncovered, until the stew thickens, about 10 minutes. Transfer 3 cups of the stew to a container and let cool. Cover and refrigerate up to 4 days for later use in Savory Stuffed Acorn Squash, opposite. Divide the remaining 7 cups of stew among 4 bowls.

PER SERVING (1¾ cups): 364 Cal, 9 g Fat, 3 g Sat Fat, 0 g Trans Fat, 100 mg Chol, 800 mg Sod, 40 g Carb, 8 g Fib, 31 g Prot, 131 mg Calc. **POINTS** value: **7.**

Savory Stuffed Acorn Squash

prep 10 MIN · microwave 15 MIN · serves 4

4   small acorn squash, about 2¼ pounds
3   cups reserved cooked Veal Stew Marsala
    (opposite)
1   cup rinsed and drained canned chickpeas
3   tablespoons chopped fresh parsley

1 Cut each squash in half through the stem end; remove the pulp and seeds. Place the squash halves, cut side down, on a large microwavable plate. Cover with plastic wrap; then prick a few holes in the plastic. Microwave on High until tender when pierced with a knife, 12 minutes.

2 Meanwhile, to make the stuffing, mix the stew, chickpeas, and parsley in a medium bowl.

3 Turn over the squash. Spoon 1 cup of the stuffing into the center of each squash half. Cover with plastic wrap; then prick a few holes in the plastic. Microwave on High until the filling is heated through, 4–5 minutes.

PER SERVING (1 stuffed squash): 329 Cal, 5 g Fat, 1 g Sat Fat, 0 g Trans Fat, 44 mg Chol, 341 mg Sod, 55 g Carb, 14 g Fib, 19 g Prot, 159 mg Calc. **POINTS** value: **6.**

make this... Veal Saltimbocca

prep 15 MIN · cook 5 MIN · serves 4 PLUS LEFTOVERS

14 fresh sage leaves

8   veal leg cutlets, about 1¼ pounds

⅛   teaspoon black pepper

8   thin slices prosciutto, about 2 ounces

½   cup low-sodium chicken broth

1½ teaspoons cornstarch

2   teaspoons olive oil

¼   cup dry white wine

Juice of ¼ lemon

1 Thinly slice 12 of the sage leaves. Place the cutlets on a sheet of plastic wrap; sprinkle with the pepper and the sliced sage. Top each cutlet with 1 slice of the prosciutto, pressing lightly to adhere.

2 Finely chop the remaining 2 sage leaves and transfer to a glass measuring cup. Stir in the broth and cornstarch until blended.

3 Heat 1 teaspoon of the oil in a large skillet over medium heat. Add 4 of the cutlets, prosciutto side down, and cook until browned, about 2 minutes. With a large spatula, carefully turn the cutlets and cook until cooked through, about 1 minute. Transfer the cutlets to a plate; cover and reserve. Repeat with the remaining 1 teaspoon of oil and 4 cutlets; transfer to another plate. Let half of the cutlets cool. Cover and refrigerate up to 2 days for later use in Saltimbocca Fennel and Orange Salad, opposite.

4 Add the wine and cook 30 seconds, scraping up the browned bits from the bottom of the skillet. Add the cornstarch mixture and cook, stirring occasionally, until reduced to ¾ cup, 2 minutes. Remove the skillet from the heat, stir in the lemon juice, and pour over the 4 reserved cutlets.

PER SERVING (1 cutlet with 3 tablespoons sauce): 128 Cal, 5 g Fat, 2 g Sat Fat, 0 g Trans Fat, 65 mg Chol, 117 mg Sod, 2 g Carb, 0 g Fib, 16 g Prot, 20 mg Calc. *POINTS* value: *3.*

Saltimbocca Fennel and Orange Salad

prep 15 MIN • cook NONE • serves 4

8 cups torn lettuce	4 reserved cooked cutlets from Veal Saltimbocca (opposite), cut into ¾-inch pieces
½ fennel bulb, thinly sliced	
1 navel orange, peeled, quartered, and sliced	½ cup low-fat red-wine vinaigrette
10 pitted kalamata olives, cut into slivers	

1 Divide the lettuce, fennel, orange, and olives among 4 plates.

2 Top each serving with ½ cup of the veal and drizzle with 2 tablespoons of the vinaigrette.

PER SERVING (1 plate): 213 Cal, 11 g Fat, 2 g Sat Fat, 0 g Trans Fat, 65 mg Chol, 508 mg Sod, 13 g Carb, 3 g Fib, 18 g Prot, 80 mg Calc. **POINTS** value: **5.**

chapter 2
Poultry Plus

Roast Chicken with Lemon and Oregano 54
Chicken Waldorf Salad 55

Chicken Marengo 56
Chicken and Asparagus Risotto 57

Apricot-Glazed Chicken 58
Chicken Cubano Panini 59

Chicken with Olives and Artichokes 60
Chicken Croquettes with Marinara Sauce 61

Argentinean-Style Chicken 62
Chicken and Shrimp Tortilla Soup 63

Vietnamese Chicken Curry 64
Thai Chicken Salad 65

Middle-Eastern Chicken 66
Chicken Samosas with Mango Chutney 67

Mango-Glazed Drumsticks 68
Chicken Egg Foo Yung 69

Chili con Pollo 70
Chicken and Penne Casserole 71

Moroccan Meatballs with Couscous 72
Spicy Meatball Pitas with Yogurt Sauce 73

Sausage and Polenta Ragoût 74
Farfalle with Sausage, Fennel, and Peppers 75

Orange Roast Turkey 76
East-West Turkey Wraps 77

Turkey Kiev Rolls 78
Crunchy Turkey Caesar Salad 79

Wasabi Dumpling Soup 80
Asian-Style Burgers 81

Sausage and Lentils 82
Smoky Sausage and Potato Salad 83

Spicy Cornish Hens with Mango Sauce 84
Jamaican Sandwiches with Mango Mayonnaise 85

Cornish Hens with Apples 86
Caribbean Cornish Hen and Sweet Potato Salad 87

Duck with Brandied Cherries 88
Savory Duck and Corn Salad 89

Grilled Duck with Spicy Grapefruit Salsa 90
Duck Hash 91

Roast Chicken with Lemon and Oregano

make this...

prep 15 MIN • roast 1 HR 30 MIN • serves 4 PLUS LEFTOVERS

1	lemon	1	(4½-pound) whole chicken
2	tablespoons chopped fresh oregano	1	acorn squash, seeded and cut lengthwise into 4 wedges
2	teaspoons olive oil		
2	garlic cloves, minced		
¾	teaspoon salt		

1 Preheat the oven to 400°F. Spray a large roasting pan with nonstick spray.

2 Grate the zest from the lemon and cut the lemon into quarters. Combine the lemon zest, oregano, oil, garlic, and ¼ teaspoon of the salt in a small bowl and mix until a paste forms. Loosen the skin from the breasts and legs of the chicken; rub the paste under the skin. Place the lemon quarters in the cavity. Tuck the wings under and tie the legs. Place, breast side up, in the prepared roasting pan.

3 Roast the chicken until an instant-read thermometer inserted in a thigh registers 180°F, 1½ hours.

4 Meanwhile, combine the squash and the remaining ½ teaspoon of salt in a large bowl; spray with nonstick spray. After the chicken has roasted 30 minutes, place the squash around the chicken and roast, turning occasionally, until tender, 30 minutes.

5 Remove the chicken from the oven; let stand 10 minutes. Discard the lemon quarters and cut the chicken in half. Let half of the chicken cool. Wrap and refrigerate up to 3 days for later use in Chicken Waldorf Salad, opposite. Carve the remaining half of chicken and serve with the squash. Discard the chicken skin before eating.

PER SERVING (½ cup sliced chicken with 1 wedge squash): 227 Cal, 8 g Fat, 2 g Sat Fat, 0 g Trans Fat, 78 mg Chol, 448 mg Sod, 13 g Carb, 4 g Fib, 27 g Prot, 63 mg Calc. **POINTS** value: **4.**

Chicken Waldorf Salad

prep 10 MIN • cook NONE • serves 4

½   cup fat-free mayonnaise

2   tablespoons mango chutney

1   tablespoon curry powder

2¼ pounds reserved cooked chicken from Roast
    Chicken with Lemon and Oregano (opposite)

2   celery stalks, diced

1   Granny Smith apple, diced

¼   cup golden raisins

2   tablespoons toasted pecans, chopped

2   scallions, thinly sliced

1 Mix the mayonnaise, chutney, and curry powder in a large bowl.

2 Remove the chicken from the bones and chop. Add to the mayonnaise mixture with the celery, apple, raisins, pecans, and scallions; toss well to coat.

PER SERVING (1¼ cups): 305 Cal, 12 g Fat, 3 g Sat Fat, 0 g Trans Fat, 82 mg Chol, 414 mg Sod, 25 g Carb, 4 g Fib, 27 g Prot, 62 mg Calc. **POINTS** value: **6.**

Chicken Marengo

prep 15 MIN • cook 45 MIN • serves 6 PLUS LEFTOVERS

1   (3½-pound) chicken, skinned and cut into 8 pieces
½   teaspoon salt
2   teaspoons olive oil
1   (10-ounce) package sliced fresh mushrooms
1   onion, thinly sliced

3   garlic cloves, minced
1   (14½-ounce) can diced tomatoes
¾   cup dry red wine
½   cup low-sodium chicken broth
8   green olives, pitted and halved

1 Sprinkle the chicken with the salt. Heat the oil in a large skillet over medium-high heat. Add the chicken and cook, turning occasionally, until browned, 6–8 minutes. Add the mushrooms, onion, and garlic. Reduce the heat and cook, stirring occasionally, until the vegetables are softened, 5 minutes. Stir in the remaining ingredients and bring to a boil. Reduce the heat; cover and simmer until the chicken is cooked through, 35 minutes.

2 Transfer 1 of the chicken breasts and 1 of the thighs to a container and let cool. Cover and refrigerate up to 3 days for later use in Chicken and Asparagus Risotto, opposite. Serve the remaining 6 pieces of chicken with the sauce.

PER SERVING (1 piece chicken with ½ cup sauce): 241 Cal, 10 g Fat, 2 g Sat Fat, 0 g Trans Fat, 84 mg Chol, 466 mg Sod, 7 g Carb, 2 g Fib, 30 g Prot, 48 mg Calc. **POINTS** value: **5.**

Chicken and Asparagus Risotto

prep 10 MIN • microwave 25 MIN • serves 4

½ cup chopped onion

2 teaspoons olive oil

1 (32-ounce) carton low-sodium chicken broth

1 cup Arborio rice

¼ cup dry vermouth

½ teaspoon salt

¼ teaspoon black pepper

1 reserved cooked chicken breast and thigh from Chicken Marengo (opposite)

1 pound fresh asparagus, trimmed and cut into 1-inch pieces

2 tablespoons grated Parmesan cheese

1 Mix the onion and oil in a medium microwavable bowl; cover with the plastic wrap. Microwave on High until the onion is softened, 2 minutes. Stir in the broth, rice, vermouth, salt, and pepper. Cover with plastic wrap; then prick a few holes in the plastic. Microwave on High 15 minutes, stirring once halfway through cooking. Uncover and microwave on High just until the rice is tender and the liquid is almost absorbed, about 5 minutes.

2 Meanwhile, remove the chicken from the bones and chop.

3 Stir the chicken and asparagus into the rice mixture. Cover with plastic wrap; then prick a few holes in the plastic. Microwave on High until the chicken is heated through and the asparagus are tender, 2–3 minutes. Stir in the cheese.

PER SERVING (1½ cups): 306 Cal, 5 g Fat, 1 g Sat Fat, 0 g Trans Fat, 18 mg Chol, 394 mg Sod, 48 g Carb, 2 g Fib, 17 g Prot, 46 mg Calc. *POINTS* value: *6.*

In the Kitchen

This recipe works equally well with short-grain white rice instead of Arborio rice.

Apricot-Glazed Chicken

prep 10 MIN • cook 10 MIN • serves 4 PLUS LEFTOVERS

¼ cup all-fruit apricot preserves

1 chipotle en adobo, minced

Grated zest and juice of 1 small lime

1 teaspoon honey

1 teaspoon ground cumin

½ teaspoon salt

6 (5-ounce) boneless skinless chicken breasts

1 To make the glaze, mix the preserves, chipotle en adobo, the lime zest and juice, and honey in a medium bowl.

2 Mix the cumin and salt in a small bowl; sprinkle over both sides of the chicken.

3 Spray a nonstick ridged grill pan with nonstick spray and set over medium-high heat. Add the chicken and cook 12 minutes, turning and brushing with the glaze every 4 minutes, until cooked through. Transfer 2 of the chicken breasts to a container and let cool. Cover and refrigerate up to 3 days for later use in Chicken Cubano Panini, opposite. Serve the remaining 4 chicken breasts.

PER SERVING (1 chicken breast): 219 Cal, 5 g Fat, 1 g Sat Fat, 0 g Trans Fat, 86 mg Chol, 364 mg Sod, 11 g Carb, 0 g Fib, 31 g Prot, 23 mg Calc. *POINTS* value: *5.*

Chicken Cubano Panini

prep 10 MIN • cook 5 MIN • serves 4

3	tablespoons light mayonnaise	4	(½-ounce) slices low-sodium ham
1	tablespoon spicy brown mustard	4	(¾-ounce) slices low-fat Swiss cheese
8	slices low-calorie multigrain bread	2	dill pickles, sliced
2	reserved cooked chicken breasts from Apricot-Glazed Chicken (opposite), thinly sliced		

1 Mix the mayonnaise and mustard in a small bowl. Spread the mixture on 4 slices of the bread. Layer the bread evenly with the chicken, ham, cheese, and pickles. Top with the remaining 4 slices of bread to make 4 sandwiches.

2 Spray a nonstick ridged grill pan with nonstick spray and set over medium-high heat or heat a panini sandwich maker according to the manufacturers' instructions. Add the sandwiches, in batches if necessary, and grill until the bread is well marked and the cheese is melted, 3–4 minutes on each side.

PER SERVING (1 sandwich): 302 Cal, 9 g Fat, 2 g Sat Fat, 0 g Trans Fat, 62 mg Chol, 1,014 mg Sod, 28 g Carb, 6 g Fib, 29 g Prot, 271 mg Calc. **POINTS** value: **6.**

◆ Filling Extra

Serve these toasty sandwiches with crisp apple wedges (1 small cut-up apple for each serving will increase the **POINTS** value by **1**).

Chicken with Olives and Artichokes

prep 10 MIN • cook 30 MIN • serves 4 PLUS LEFTOVERS

6 **(5-ounce) boneless skinless chicken breasts**	**¼** **cup low-sodium chicken broth**
½ **teaspoon salt**	**Juice of ½ lemon**
½ **teaspoon black pepper**	**8** **kalamata olives, pitted and chopped**
2 **teaspoons olive oil**	
1 **(8.5-ounce) can artichoke hearts, drained and quartered**	**2** **garlic cloves, minced**
	1 **tablespoon chopped fresh basil**

1 Sprinkle the chicken with the salt and the pepper. Heat the oil in a large skillet over medium-high heat. Add the chicken and cook until lightly browned, about 3 minutes on each side. Stir in the artichokes, broth, lemon juice, olives, and garlic; bring to a boil. Reduce the heat; cover and cook until the flavors are blended and the chicken is cooked through, 5 minutes.

2 Transfer 2 of the chicken breasts to a container and let cool. Cover and refrigerate up to 3 days for later use in Chicken Croquettes with Marinara Sauce, opposite. Remove the skillet from the heat and stir in the basil. Serve the remaining 4 chicken breasts with the sauce.

PER SERVING (1 chicken breast with ¼ cup sauce): 234 Cal, 8 g Fat, 2 g Sat Fat, 0 g Trans Fat, 86 mg Chol, 591 mg Sod, 7 g Carb, 3 g Fib, 33 g Prot, 50 mg Calc. *POINTS* value: *5.*

...then this!

Chicken Croquettes with Marinara Sauce

prep 10 MIN • bake/cook 25 MIN • serves 4

2 reserved cooked chicken breasts from Chicken with Olives and Artichokes (opposite), chopped

1 (8.8-ounce) package cooked brown-and-wild-rice blend (about 1¾ cups)

⅔ cup shredded part-skim mozzarella cheese

½ cup frozen peas, thawed

3 tablespoons fat-free mayonnaise

2 tablespoons grated Parmesan cheese

2 large egg whites

6 tablespoons plain dried bread crumbs

1 cup marinara sauce

1 Preheat the oven to 400°F. Spray a large baking sheet with nonstick spray.

2 Pulse the chicken and rice in a food processor until finely chopped; transfer to a large bowl. Stir in the mozzarella, peas, mayonnaise, and Parmesan. With moistened hands, form into 8 (3-inch) logs. Whisk the egg whites in a medium bowl. Spread the bread crumbs on a sheet of wax paper. Dip each log into the egg whites, then roll in the crumbs.

3 Place the croquettes on the prepared baking sheet and spray lightly with nonstick spray. Bake until golden, about 25 minutes.

4 Meanwhile, heat the marinara sauce in a small saucepan over medium heat until hot, 5 minutes. Serve the croquettes with the sauce.

PER SERVING (2 croquettes with ¼ cup sauce): 343 Cal, 10 g Fat, 4 g Sat Fat, 0 g Trans Fat, 50 mg Chol, 1,024 mg Sod, 37 g Carb, 4 g Fib, 26 g Prot, 231 mg Calc. **POINTS** value: **7.**

Argentinean-Style Chicken

prep 15 MIN • cook 20 MIN • serves 4 PLUS LEFTOVERS

2	baking potatoes, peeled and sliced ¼-inch thick	½	cup chopped fresh basil
4	small carrots, halved crosswise	3	tablespoons red-wine vinegar
2	cups low-sodium chicken broth	1	tablespoon extra-virgin olive oil
6	(5-ounce) boneless skinless chicken breasts	2	garlic cloves, peeled
½	cup chopped fresh cilantro	½	teaspoon salt

1 Bring the potatoes, carrots, and broth to a boil in a large skillet. Reduce the heat; cover and simmer until the vegetables are crisp-tender, 10 minutes. Add the chicken and bring to a boil. Reduce the heat; cover and simmer until the chicken is cooked through and the vegetables are tender, 10–12 minutes.

2 Meanwhile, to make the sauce, put the cilantro, basil, vinegar, oil, garlic, and salt in a food processor and pulse until smooth.

3 Discard the cooking liquid. Transfer 2 of the chicken breasts to a container and let cool. Cover and refrigerate up to 3 days for later use in Chicken and Shrimp Tortilla Soup, opposite. Serve the remaining 4 chicken breasts with the vegetables and sauce.

PER SERVING (1 chicken breast with ½ cup vegetables and 2 tablespoons sauce): 354 Cal, 8 g Fat, 2 g Sat Fat, 0 g Trans Fat, 86 mg Chol, 408 mg Sod, 34 g Carb, 4 g Fib, 35 g Prot, 50 mg Calc. **POINTS** value: **7.**

Chicken and Shrimp Tortilla Soup

prep 5 MIN • cook 10 MIN • serves 4

1 (32-ounce) carton low-sodium chicken broth

1 (10-ounce) can diced tomatoes with green chiles

½ pound large peeled and deveined shrimp

2 cups chopped fresh spinach

2 reserved cooked chicken breasts from Argentinean-Style Chicken (opposite), chopped

¼ cup shredded low-fat cheddar cheese

1 corn tortilla, cut into thin strips

1 Bring the broth, tomatoes, shrimp, and spinach to a boil in a large saucepan. Reduce the heat; cover and simmer just until the shrimp turns opaque in the center and the spinach is wilted, 3 minutes.

2 Add the chicken and cook, uncovered, stirring occasionally, until heated through, 3 minutes. Serve topped with cheese and tortilla strips.

PER SERVING (1¾ cups soup with 1 tablespoon cheese and 1 tablespoon tortilla strips): 200 Cal, 5 g Fat, 1 g Sat Fat, 0 g Trans Fat, 125 mg Chol, 391 mg Sod, 8 g Carb, 1 g Fib, 32 g Prot, 122 mg Calc. *POINTS* value: *4.*

◆ Filling Extra

For another *2 POINTS* value, top each serving of the soup with ¼ diced avocado in addition to the cheese and tortilla strips.

Vietnamese Chicken Curry

prep 15 MIN • cook 30 MIN • serves 4 PLUS LEFTOVERS

1½ **pounds boneless skinless chicken thighs, cut into 2-inch pieces**

2 **teaspoons canola oil**

1 **onion, thinly sliced**

2 **tablespoons minced peeled fresh ginger**

2 **garlic cloves, minced**

1 **tablespoon garam masala**

1 **tablespoon packed brown sugar**

½ **pound small red potatoes, scrubbed and halved**

1 **(14½-ounce) can diced tomatoes, drained**

1 **cup low-sodium chicken broth**

½ **cup light (reduced-fat) coconut milk**

¼ **cup chopped fresh cilantro**

1 Spray a large nonstick skillet with nonstick spray and set over medium heat. Add the chicken and cook, stirring occasionally, until browned, 5–6 minutes. Transfer the chicken to a plate and reserve.

2 Heat the oil in the skillet over medium-high heat. Add the onion and cook, stirring occasionally, until softened, 5 minutes. Add the ginger, garlic, garam masala, and brown sugar; cook, stirring constantly, until fragrant, 1 minute. Add the chicken, potatoes, tomatoes, and broth; bring to a boil. Reduce the heat; cover and simmer until the chicken is cooked through and the potatoes are fork-tender, 15 minutes.

3 Remove the skillet from the heat; stir in the coconut milk and cilantro. With a slotted spoon, transfer 2 cups of the chicken to a container and let cool. Cover and refrigerate up to 3 days for later use in Thai Chicken Salad, opposite. Serve the remaining chicken with the vegetables and sauce.

PER SERVING (1¼ cups): 278 Cal, 11 g Fat, 3 g Sat Fat, 0 g Trans Fat, 53 mg Chol, 227 mg Sod, 24 g Carb, 4 g Fib, 22 g Prot, 86 mg Calc. **POINTS** value: **6.**

Thai Chicken Salad

prep 10 MIN • cook NONE • serves 4

1	tablespoon rice vinegar	1	(10-ounce) bag broccoli slaw
1	tablespoon low-sodium soy sauce	1	(4-ounce) bag watercress, chopped
1	tablespoon mirin	½	cup chopped fresh cilantro
1	tablespoon minced peeled fresh ginger	3	tablespoons chopped dry-roasted peanuts
2	cups reserved cooked chicken from Vietnamese Chicken Curry (opposite), chopped		

1 To make the dressing, whisk the vinegar, soy sauce, mirin, and ginger in a large bowl until blended.

2 Add the chicken, broccoli slaw, watercress, and cilantro; toss to coat. Sprinkle with the peanuts.

PER SERVING (1½ cups): 217 Cal, 11 g Fat, 3 g Sat Fat, 0 g Trans Fat, 55 mg Chol, 274 mg Sod, 7 g Carb, 3 g Fib, 23 g Prot, 94 mg Calc. *POINTS* value: *5.*

make this...

Middle-Eastern Chicken

prep 10 MIN • cook 20 MIN • serves 4 PLUS LEFTOVERS

½ teaspoon cinnamon

½ teaspoon ground cumin

¾ teaspoon salt

6 (¼-pound) boneless skinless chicken thighs, cut into 2-inch pieces

1 (14½-ounce) can diced tomatoes, drained

1 tablespoon tomato paste

1 tablespoon minced peeled fresh ginger

2 garlic cloves, minced

¼ cup chopped fresh cilantro

2 tablespoons toasted pine nuts

1 Combine the cinnamon, cumin, and ¼ teaspoon of the salt in a medium bowl. Add the chicken and toss to coat.

2 Spray a large nonstick skillet with nonstick spray and set over medium-high heat. Add the chicken and cook until browned, 3–4 minutes on each side. Stir in the tomatoes, tomato paste, ginger, garlic, and the remaining ½ teaspoon of salt; bring to a boil. Reduce the heat; cover and simmer until the chicken is cooked through and the flavors are blended, 10–12 minutes.

3 Remove the skillet from the heat. With a slotted spoon, transfer 1 cup of the chicken to a container and let cool. Cover and refrigerate up to 3 days for later use in Chicken Samosas with Mango Chutney, opposite. Serve the remaining 4 cups of chicken topped with the cilantro and pine nuts.

PER SERVING (1 cup): 240 Cal, 12 g Fat, 3 g Sat Fat, 0 g Trans Fat, 71 mg Chol, 539 mg Sod, 7 g Carb, 2 g Fib, 26 g Prot, 68 mg Calc. **POINTS** value: **5.**

...then this!

Chicken Samosas with Mango Chutney

prep 20 MIN • cook/bake 20 MIN • serves 5

1	cup refrigerated ready-to-cook mashed potatoes
1	tablespoon curry powder
½	teaspoon salt
1	cup reserved cooked chicken from Middle-Eastern Chicken (opposite), chopped
¾	cup frozen peas, thawed
1	(7½-ounce) can refrigerated buttermilk biscuits
5	tablespoons mango chutney

1 Preheat the oven to 450°F. Spray a large baking sheet with nonstick spray.

2 To make the filling, spray a large nonstick skillet with nonstick spray and set over medium-high heat. Add the potatoes, curry powder, and salt; cook, stirring occasionally, until browned, 3–4 minutes. Add the chicken and peas; cook, stirring occasionally, until heated through, 5 minutes. Let cool slightly.

3 On a lightly floured surface, roll each biscuit into a 4½-inch round. Spoon 1 heaping tablespoon of the filling evenly onto the center of each round. Fold the dough over the filling and press the edges firmly to seal.

4 Place the samosas on the prepared baking sheet and bake until golden, about 12 minutes. Serve with the chutney.

PER SERVING (2 samosas with 1 tablespoon chutney): 339 Cal, 9 g Fat, 2 g Sat Fat, 1 g Trans Fat, 36 mg Chol, 1,091 mg Sod, 47 g Carb, 4 g Fib, 18 g Prot, 42 mg Calc. **POINTS** value: **7.**

make this...

Mango-Glazed Drumsticks

prep 15 MIN • cook/grill 40 MIN • serves 4 PLUS LEFTOVERS

1 mango, seeded, peeled, and cubed	¾ teaspoon salt
¼ cup Sriracha (Thai-style hot chile sauce)	10 (¼-pound) chicken drumsticks, skinned
Juice of ½ lime	1 red bell pepper, thinly sliced
1 tablespoon honey	2 scallions, thinly sliced

1 Spray the grill rack with nonstick spray and prepare a medium hot fire.

2 To make the glaze, puree the mango, Sriracha, lime juice, honey, and ¼ teaspoon of the salt in a food processor. Transfer the puree to a small saucepan and bring to a boil over medium-high heat. Reduce the heat and simmer until slightly thickened, 5 minutes. Remove the saucepan from the heat.

3 Sprinkle the drumsticks with the remaining ½ teaspoon of salt. Place the drumsticks on the grill rack and grill, covered, turning once or twice, 20 minutes. Uncover the grill and continue to grill the chicken, brushing with the glaze and turning, until cooked through, 10 minutes.

4 Transfer 2 of the drumsticks to a container and let cool. Cover and refrigerate up to 3 days for later use in Chicken Egg Foo Yung, opposite. Sprinkle the remaining 8 drumsticks with the bell pepper and scallions.

PER SERVING (2 drumsticks): 212 Cal, 4 g Fat, 1 g Sat Fat, 0 g Trans Fat, 102 mg Chol, 612 mg Sod, 16 g Carb, 2 g Fib, 27 g Prot, 39 mg Calc. *POINTS* value: *4.*

Chicken Egg Foo Yung

prep 10 MIN • cook 15 MIN • serves 4

2 reserved cooked chicken drumsticks from Mango-Glazed Drumsticks (opposite)	**1** teaspoon Asian (dark) sesame oil
1½ cups fat-free egg substitute	**2** teaspoons canola oil
1 tablespoon low-sodium soy sauce	**1** (12-ounce) package frozen Asian-style vegetables, thawed and patted dry
1 tablespoon chopped scallions	

1 Remove the chicken from the bones and chop. Whisk the egg substitute, soy sauce, scallions, and sesame oil in a large bowl until blended.

2 Heat the canola oil in a large skillet over medium-high heat. Add the vegetables and cook, stirring occasionally, until softened, 6 minutes. Stir in the chicken and top evenly with the egg mixture. Reduce the heat and cook, lifting the edges frequently with a spatula, until the underside is set, 3–4 minutes. Cover and cook until the top is set, 6–8 minutes. Cut into 4 wedges.

PER SERVING (1 wedge): 155 Cal, 5 g Fat, 1 g Sat Fat, 0 g Trans Fat, 25 mg Chol, 465 mg Sod, 11 g Carb, 3 g Fib, 18 g Prot, 183 mg Calc. **POINTS** value: **3.**

♦ Filling Extra

Love your greens? A few minutes before the vegetables are softened in step 2, stir in 4 cups baby spinach and cook just until wilted.

Chili con Pollo

prep 15 MIN • cook 55 MIN • serves 4 PLUS LEFTOVERS

2	teaspoons olive oil
1½	pounds ground skinless chicken breast
¼	cup chili powder
2	teaspoons ground cumin
¾	teaspoon salt
1	onion, chopped
3	garlic cloves, minced

1	(28-ounce) can crushed tomatoes
1	cup salsa verde
½	cup water
2	zucchini, diced
1	yellow squash, diced
¼	cup shredded low-fat cheddar cheese

1 Heat the oil in a Dutch oven over medium-high heat. Add the chicken, chili powder, cumin, and salt; brown the chicken, breaking it up with a wooden spoon, about 5 minutes. Add the onion and garlic; cook, stirring frequently, until the onion is softened, 6 minutes.

2 Stir in the tomatoes, salsa, water, zucchini, and yellow squash; bring to a boil. Reduce the heat; cover and simmer, stirring occasionally, until the vegetables soften and the flavors are blended, 45 minutes.

3 Transfer half of the chili (4 cups) to a container and let cool. Cover and refrigerate up to 3 days for later use in Chicken and Penne Casserole, opposite. Serve the remaining 4 cups of chili with the cheese.

PER SERVING (1 cup chili with 1 tablespoon cheese): 181 Cal, 5 g Fat, 1 g Sat Fat, 0 g Trans Fat, 53 mg Chol, 572 mg Sod, 12 g Carb, 4 g Fib, 23 g Prot, 124 mg Calc. **POINTS** value: **3.**

Chicken and Penne Casserole

prep 10 MIN • cook/bake 40 MIN • serves 4

½   **pound whole-wheat penne**

4   **cups reserved cooked Chili con Pollo (opposite)**

⅔   **cup shredded low-fat cheddar cheese**

1 Preheat the oven to 375°F. Spray a 9-inch square baking dish with nonstick spray.

2 Cook the penne according to the package directions, omitting the salt if desired. Drain.

3 Toss the penne and chili in a large bowl; spoon into the prepared baking dish. Sprinkle with the cheese and bake until hot and the cheese melts, 20–25 minutes.

PER SERVING (generous 1½ cups): 399 Cal, 7 g Fat, 2 g Sat Fat, 0 g Trans Fat, 55 mg Chol, 935 mg Sod, 54 g Carb, 8 g Fib, 34 g Prot, 234 mg Calc. **POINTS** value: **8.**

♦ Filling Extra

To add more fiber and bulk to both the Chili con Pollo and the Chicken and Penne Casserole, add 2 (15½-ounce) cans of rinsed and drained kidney beans when preparing the chili recipe in step 3 and heat through. The per-serving **POINTS** value of each dish will increase by **1.**

make this...

Moroccan Meatballs with Couscous

prep 20 MIN • cook 15 MIN • serves 4 PLUS LEFTOVERS

1   (10-ounce) box whole-wheat couscous
1½ pounds ground skinless chicken
12 whole pitted dried plums
1   shallot, coarsely chopped
1   (1-inch) piece ginger, peeled and chopped

2   garlic cloves
1   teaspoon cinnamon
½   teaspoon ground cumin
2   teaspoons canola oil
Grated zest of 1 lemon

1 Cook the couscous according to the package directions.

2 Meanwhile, put the chicken, plums, shallot, ginger, garlic, cinnamon, and cumin in a food processor and pulse until finely chopped. Transfer the mixture to a large bowl. With damp hands, form into 20 (1½-inch) meatballs.

3 Heat the oil in a large skillet over medium-high heat. Add the meatballs and cook, in batches if necessary, until cooked through, 10–12 minutes. Transfer 8 of the meatballs to a plate and let cool. Cover and refrigerate up to 3 days for later use in Spicy Meatball Pitas with Yogurt Sauce, opposite.

4 Fluff the couscous with a fork and transfer to a platter. Spoon the remaining 12 meatballs over the top and sprinkle with the lemon zest.

PER SERVING (3 meatballs with ¾ cup couscous): 374 Cal, 8 g Fat, 2 g Sat Fat, 0 g Trans Fat, 65 mg Chol, 616 mg Sod, 49 g Carb, 8 g Fib, 29 g Prot, 65 mg Calc. **POINTS** value: **7.**

Spicy Meatball Pitas with Yogurt Sauce

prep 10 MIN • cook NONE • serves 4

1	cup plain fat-free Greek yogurt
¼	cup peeled, seeded, and finely diced cucumber
2	tablespoons chopped fresh dill
1	garlic clove, minced
	Juice of ¼ lemon

4	(6-inch) whole-wheat pita breads
2	cups packed thinly sliced romaine lettuce
8	reserved cooked meatballs from Moroccan Meatballs with Couscous (opposite), halved
2	small tomatoes, each cut into 4 wedges

1 To make the sauce, mix the yogurt, cucumber, dill, garlic, and lemon juice in a small bowl until blended.

2 Cut the top third off of each pita and discard. Stuff each pita with ¼ cup of the lettuce, 4 meatball halves, and 2 tomato wedges. Serve topped with the sauce.

PER SERVING (1 stuffed pita with 3 tablespoons sauce): 280 Cal, 6 g Fat, 1 g Sat Fat, 0 g Trans Fat, 45 mg Chol, 289 mg Sod, 36 g Carb, 5 g Fib, 22 g Prot, 161 mg Calc. **POINTS** value: **5.**

In the Kitchen

If you'd like to serve these sandwiches hot instead of cold, place the meatballs in a microwavable dish, cover with plastic wrap; then prick a few holes in the plastic. Microwave on High until hot, 2 minutes, stirring once halfway through cooking. Microwave the pita according to the package directions.

make this...

Sausage and Polenta Ragoût

prep 10 MIN • cook 20 MIN • serves 4 PLUS LEFTOVERS

1	teaspoon olive oil	1	cup marinara sauce
6	fully-cooked chicken sausage links (about 1 pound)	½	cup dry white wine
		8	pitted kalamata olives, chopped
1	(8-ounce) package sliced fresh mushrooms	1	teaspoon chopped fresh rosemary
1	onion, thinly sliced	1	(16-ounce) tube refrigerated fat-free plain polenta, cut into 8 rounds
1	garlic clove, minced		
¼	teaspoon salt		

1 Heat the oil in a large skillet over medium-high heat. Add the sausages, mushrooms, onion, garlic, and salt; cook, stirring occasionally, until the vegetables are tender, 8 minutes.

2 With tongs, transfer the sausages to a cutting board. Transfer 3 of the sausages to a container and let cool. Cover and refrigerate up to 3 days for later use in Farfalle with Sausage, Fennel, and Peppers, opposite.

3 Slice the remaining 3 sausages and return to the skillet. Add the marinara sauce, wine, olives, and rosemary; bring to a boil. Reduce the heat and simmer, stirring occasionally, until the flavors are blended and the sauce thickens slightly, about 10 minutes.

4 Meanwhile, spray the broiler rack with nonstick spray and preheat the broiler. Broil the polenta 4 inches from the heat until lightly browned and heated through, about 3 minutes. Transfer the polenta to a platter and top with the ragoût.

PER SERVING (¾ cup ragoût with 2 slices polenta): 287 Cal, 11 g Fat, 3 g Sat Fat, 0 g Trans Fat, 33 mg Chol, 1,156 mg Sod, 34 g Carb, 3 g Fib, 14 g Prot, 45 mg Calc. **POINTS** value: **6.**

74 POULTRY PLUS

...then this!

Farfalle with Sausage, Fennel, and Peppers

prep 10 MIN • cook 20 MIN • serves 4

4	ounces whole-wheat farfalle
1	teaspoon olive oil
3	reserved cooked chicken sausages from Sausage and Polenta Ragoût (opposite), sliced
4	Italian frying peppers, cut into 2-inch chunks
1	fennel bulb, cut into 2-inch chunks

1	garlic clove, minced
¼	teaspoon salt
½	cup dry white wine
¼	cup fresh chopped basil
3	tablespoons grated Parmesan cheese
	Fresh basil leaves, for garnish

1 Cook the farfalle according to the package directions, omitting the salt if desired.

2 Meanwhile, heat the oil in a large skillet over medium-high heat. Add the sausages, peppers, fennel, garlic, and salt. Stir in the wine and bring to a boil. Reduce the heat and simmer, stirring occasionally, until the sausages are browned and the vegetables are tender, about 8 minutes.

3 Drain the farfalle, reserving ¼ cup of the cooking liquid. Add the farfalle and the cooking liquid to the sausage mixture, stirring until blended. Stir in the chopped basil and cheese. Garnish with the basil leaves.

PER SERVING (1 cup): 278 Cal, 10 g Fat, 3 g Sat Fat, 0 g Trans Fat, 36 mg Chol, 724 mg Sod, 31 g Carb, 5 g Fib, 17 g Prot, 126 mg Calc. **POINTS** value: **6.**

Orange Roast Turkey

prep 15 MIN • roast 2 HRS • serves 6 PLUS LEFTOVERS

1 tablespoon grated orange zest	1 (4½-pound) turkey breast with ribs
2 tablespoons chopped fresh rosemary	2 sweet potatoes, peeled and cut into 2-inch chunks
3 teaspoons olive oil	1 navel orange, cut into wedges
1 teaspoon salt	

1 Preheat the oven to 375°F. Spray a large roasting pan with nonstick spray. Stir the orange zest, 1 tablespoon of the rosemary, 1 teaspoon of the oil, and ½ teaspoon of the salt in a small bowl until a paste forms. Loosen the skin around the turkey breast by running your fingers between the skin and the meat, starting at the tips of the breast halves. Once the skin is loosened, divide the paste between the 2 halves and spread it on the meat, patting the skin back in place.

2 Place the turkey breast, skin side up, in the prepared pan and roast until an instant-read thermometer inserted into the center registers 165°F, 2 hours.

3 Meanwhile, mix the potatoes, orange, and the remaining 1 tablespoon of rosemary, 2 teaspoons of oil, and ½ teaspoon of salt in a large bowl. After the turkey breast has roasted 1½ hours, place the potato mixture around the turkey breast and roast, turning occasionally, until the potatoes are fork-tender, 30 minutes.

4 Transfer the turkey breast to a cutting board and let stand 10 minutes. Discard the ribs from the turkey and cut it crosswise in half. Transfer half of the turkey to a container and let cool. Cover and refrigerate up to 3 days for later use in East-West Turkey Wraps, opposite. Cut the remaining half of turkey into 12 slices and serve with the potato mixture. Remove the skin before eating.

PER SERVING (2 slices turkey with ½ cup potato mixture): 211 Cal, 5 g Fat, 1 g Sat Fat, 0 g Trans Fat, 67 mg Chol, 318 mg Sod, 24 g Carb, 3 g Fib, 16 g Prot, 49 mg Calc. **POINTS** value: **4.**

East-West Turkey Wraps

prep 10 MIN • cook 5 MIN • serves 6

2¼ pounds reserved cooked turkey from Orange Roast Turkey (opposite), skinned and shredded

¼ cup hoisin sauce

6 (8-inch) whole-wheat tortillas

¼ cup shredded carrot

¼ cup sliced scallions

1 Mix the turkey and hoisin sauce in a large bowl.

2 Set a large skillet over medium heat. Add the tortillas and cook until hot, 30 seconds on each side.

3 Spoon ½ cup of the turkey mixture onto each tortilla. Top evenly with the carrot and scallions; roll up. Cut each roll in half on a slight diagonal.

PER SERVING (1 wrap): 265 Cal, 3 g Fat, 1 g Sat Fat, 0 g Trans Fat, 89 mg Chol, 521 mg Sod, 23 g Carb, 4 g Fib, 35 g Prot, 34 mg Calc. **POINTS** value: **5.**

◆ Filling Extra

Top the wraps evenly with 1 bunch trimmed watercress in addition to the carrot and scallions before rolling them up in step 3.

Turkey Kiev Rolls

prep 15 MIN • bake 30 MIN • serves 4 PLUS LEFTOVERS

2 tablespoons light stick butter	6 (4-ounce) turkey cutlets, lightly pounded
2 tablespoons chopped fresh dill	2 tablespoons Dijon mustard
Grated zest and juice of ½ lemon	2 cups baby arugula
¼ teaspoon salt	1 cup bite-size pieces radicchio
½ cup + 2 tablespoons panko bread crumbs	3 tablespoons light balsamic vinaigrette

1 Preheat the oven to 425°F. Spray a baking sheet with nonstick spray.

2 Mix the butter, dill, lemon zest and juice, and salt in a small bowl. Spread the bread crumbs on a sheet of wax paper. Place the cutlets on a work surface with the short ends facing you. Spoon 1½ teaspoons of the butter mixture in the center of each cutlet. Starting at each short end, roll up and secure with a toothpick. Brush the rolls with the mustard, then roll in the crumbs to coat completely.

3 Place the rolls on the prepared baking sheet and lightly spray with nonstick spray. Bake until the rolls are cooked through, 30 minutes.

4 Transfer 2 of the rolls to a container and let cool. Cover and refrigerate up to 3 days for later use in Crunchy Turkey Caesar Salad, opposite. Mix the arugula and radicchio in a medium bowl. Add the vinaigrette and toss to coat. Serve with the remaining 4 rolls.

PER SERVING (1 roll with ¾ cup salad): 197 Cal, 6 g Fat, 2 g Sat Fat, 0 g Trans Fat, 80 mg Chol, 504 mg Sod, 7 g Carb, 1 g Fib, 28 g Prot, 47 mg Calc. **POINTS** value: **4.**

Crunchy Turkey Caesar Salad

prep 5 MIN • cook NONE • serves 4

1	heart of romaine lettuce, coarsely chopped
3	tablespoons light Caesar dressing
1	tablespoon grated Parmesan cheese

2	reserved cooked turkey from Turkey Kiev Rolls (opposite), cut into 8 (¼-inch-thick) slices
½	cup whole-wheat croutons

1 Toss the lettuce, dressing, and cheese in a large bowl. Divide evenly among 4 plates.

2 Top each plate evenly with the sliced turkey and sprinkle with the croutons.

PER SERVING (1⅓ cups salad with 2 slices turkey roll and 2 tablespoons croutons): 142 Cal, 5 g Fat, 2 g Sat Fat, 0 g Trans Fat, 54 mg Chol, 324 mg Sod, 8 g Carb, 1 g Fib, 15 g Prot, 44 mg Calc. *POINTS* value: *3.*

◆ Filling Extra

Add 1 cup each cherry tomatoes and shredded carrots to the salad in step 1.

Wasabi Dumpling Soup

prep 25 MIN • cook 20 MIN • serves 4 PLUS LEFTOVERS

1¼ **pounds ground skinless turkey breast**

6 **scallions, finely chopped**

3 **tablespoons low-sodium soy sauce**

2 **tablespoons minced peeled fresh ginger**

1 **tablespoon wasabi powder**

2 **teaspoons Asian (dark) sesame oil**

16 **(3-inch) square wonton wrappers**

1 **(32-ounce) carton low-sodium chicken broth**

¼ **pound baby bok choy, chopped**

1 **(8-ounce) can bamboo shoots, drained**

1 Mix the turkey, scallions, 2 tablespoons of the soy sauce, 1 tablespoon of the ginger, the wasabi powder, and oil in a medium bowl just until blended. Transfer 2 cups of the turkey mixture to a container. Cover and refrigerate up to 2 days for later use in Asian-Style Burgers, opposite.

2 Arrange 8 wonton wrappers on a work surface. Place 1 teaspoon of the remaining turkey mixture in the center of each wrapper. Moisten the edges of each wrapper with water and pull one of the top corners diagonally over the filling to make a triangle. Press the edges firmly to seal. Place the filled dumplings on a baking sheet and cover with damp paper towels. Repeat with the remaining filling and wrappers, making a total of 16 dumplings.

3 Meanwhile, bring the broth and the remaining 1 tablespoon of soy sauce and 1 tablespoon of ginger to a boil in a large saucepan.

4 Add the dumplings, bok choy, and bamboo shoots to the broth mixture. Reduce the heat and simmer, stirring occasionally, until the dumplings are cooked through and the bok choy is tender, about 10 minutes.

PER SERVING (1 cup soup with 4 dumplings): 185 Cal, 3 g Fat, 1 g Sat Fat, 0 g Trans Fat, 35 mg Chol, 310 mg Sod, 25 g Carb, 2 g Fib, 16 g Prot, 57 mg Calc. **POINTS** value: **4.**

Asian-Style Burgers

prep 40 MIN • cook 15 MIN • serves 4

2 cups reserved turkey mixture from Wasabi Dumpling Soup (opposite)

¼ cup panko bread crumbs

1 tablespoon teriyaki sauce

2 teaspoons canola oil

¾ pound fresh shiitake mushrooms, tough stems removed, thinly sliced

4 scallions, cut into 3-inch pieces

¼ teaspoon salt

4 whole-grain buns, split and toasted

1 Mix the turkey mixture, bread crumbs, and teriyaki sauce in a large bowl just until blended. With damp hands, form the mixture into 4 (1-inch-thick) burgers. Cover and refrigerate 30 minutes.

2 Spray a ridged grill pan with nonstick spray; set over medium-high heat. Cook the burgers, turning occasionally, until an instant-read thermometer inserted into side of each burger registers 165°F, 15 minutes.

3 Meanwhile, heat the oil in a large skillet over medium-high heat. Add the mushrooms, scallions, and salt. Cook, stirring occasionally, until tender, 5 minutes. Spoon over the burgers. Serve in the buns.

PER SERVING (1 burger with ½ cup vegetables): 325 Cal, 6 g Fat, 1 g Sat Fat, 0 g Trans Fat, 75 mg Chol, 820 mg Sod, 35 g Carb, 7 g Fib, 34 g Prot, 101 mg Calc. **POINTS** value: **6.**

make this... # Sausage and Lentils

prep 10 MIN • cook 50 MIN • serves 4 PLUS LEFTOVERS

2	**teaspoons canola oil**
1	**onion, thinly sliced**
1	**cup lentils, picked over and rinsed**
1½	**pounds turkey kielbasa, cut into 4-inch pieces**
3	**cups low-sodium chicken broth**

1 Heat the oil in a large nonstick skillet over medium-high heat. Add the onion and cook, stirring occasionally, until tender, 8 minutes. Stir in the lentils. Place the kielbasa on top of the lentils. Add the broth and bring to a boil. Reduce the heat; cover and simmer, stirring occasionally, until the lentils are tender, about 40 minutes. Remove from the heat.

2 With tongs, transfer 2 cups of the kielbasa pieces to a container and let cool. Cover and refrigerate up to 3 days for later use in Smoky Sausage and Potato Salad, opposite. Serve the remaining 2 cups of kielbasa with the lentils.

PER SERVING (½ cup kielbasa with ½ cup lentils): 337 Cal, 11 g Fat, 3 g Sat Fat, 0 g Trans Fat, 44 mg Chol, 907 mg Sod, 32 g Carb, 8 g Fib, 28 g Prot, 47 mg Calc. **POINTS** value: **7.**

...then this!

Smoky Sausage and Potato Salad

prep 10 MIN • cook 30 MIN • serves 4

1	pound baby Yukon Gold potatoes, halved
2	tablespoons tarragon vinegar
2	teaspoons olive oil
1	teaspoon whole-grain Dijon mustard
¼	teaspoon salt

2	cups reserved cooked turkey kielbasa from Sausage and Lentils (opposite), cut into 1-inch pieces
1	green bell pepper, diced
1	celery stalk, diced
2	tablespoons chopped fresh parsley

1 Bring the potatoes and enough cold water to cover to a boil in a medium saucepan. Reduce the heat; cover and simmer until the potatoes are fork-tender, 20 minutes. Drain and transfer the potatoes to a large bowl and let cool 10 minutes.

2 Meanwhile, to make the dressing, whisk the vinegar, oil, mustard, and salt in a small bowl until blended.

3 Add the kielbasa, bell pepper, celery, and parsley to the potatoes; stir to mix. Drizzle with the dressing and toss well to coat.

PER SERVING (1 cup): 240 Cal, 10 g Fat, 2 g Sat Fat, 0 g Trans Fat, 44 mg Chol, 860 mg Sod, 22 g Carb, 3 g Fib, 15 g Prot, 43 mg Calc. **POINTS** value: **5.**

◆ Filling Extra

Top each serving of either the Sausage and Lentils or the Smoky Sausage and Potato Salad with ¼ cup shredded fat-free Swiss cheese and up the **POINTS** value by **1.** To add more veggies to the potato salad, serve it on a platter lined with 4 cups of sturdy greens—like watercress or romaine.

make this...

Spicy Cornish Hens with Mango Sauce

prep 15 MIN • roast/cook 40 MIN • serves 4 PLUS LEFTOVERS

3 **(1¼-pound) Cornish game hens, skinned**	1 **mango, peeled, seeded, and cubed**
2 **tablespoons jerk seasoning**	¼ **cup cider vinegar**
2 **teaspoons canola oil**	2 **tablespoons packed brown sugar**
1 **medium onion, chopped**	¼ **teaspoon salt**
1 **tablespoon minced peeled fresh ginger**	

1 Preheat the oven to 400°F. Spray a large roasting pan with nonstick spray.

2 Tie the legs of each hen together with kitchen string and rub evenly with the seasoning. Place the hens, breast side up, in the prepared roasting pan. Roast until an instant-read thermometer inserted into a thigh registers 180°F, about 40 minutes.

3 Meanwhile, to make the sauce, heat the oil in a medium saucepan over medium-high heat. Add the onion and ginger; cook, stirring occasionally, until tender, 5 minutes. Add the mango, vinegar, brown sugar, and salt; bring to a boil. Reduce the heat and simmer until the sauce thickens slightly, about 8 minutes.

4 Transfer 1 of the hens and ¼ cup of the sauce to separate containers and let cool. Cover and refrigerate up to 3 days for later use in Jamaican Sandwiches with Mango Mayonnaise, opposite. Cut the remaining 2 hens in half. Serve with the remaining 1 cup sauce.

PER SERVING (½ hen with ¼ cup sauce): 252 Cal, 7 g Fat, 1 g Sat Fat, 0 g Trans Fat, 132 mg Chol, 244 mg Sod, 17 g Carb, 2 g Fib, 30 g Prot, 49 mg Calc. **POINTS** value: **5.**

...then this!

Jamaican Sandwiches with Mango Mayonnaise

prep 10 MIN • cook NONE • serves 4

1 reserved cooked Cornish hen and ¼ cup reserved sauce from Spicy Cornish Hens with Mango Sauce (opposite)	**8** slices low-calorie whole-grain bread
2 tablespoons fat-free mayonnaise	**4** green leaf lettuce leaves
Juice of ½ small lime	**1** large tomato, cut into 8 slices
	½ red onion, thinly sliced

1 Remove the meat from the bones of the hen and thinly slice.

2 To make the mayonnaise, mix the sauce, mayonnaise, and lime juice in a small bowl.

3 Spread the mayonnaise evenly on 4 slices of the bread. Layer each slice with one-fourth of the hen, 1 lettuce leaf, 2 tomato slices, and one-fourth of the onion. Top with the remaining bread to make 4 sandwiches.

PER SERVING (1 sandwich): 245 Cal, 5 g Fat, 1 g Sat Fat, 0 g Trans Fat, 67 mg Chol, 364 mg Sod, 29 g Carb, 5 g Fib, 22 g Prot, 87 mg Calc. **POINTS** value: **5.**

make this...

Cornish Hens with Apples

prep 15 MIN • roast 1 HR • serves 4 PLUS LEFTOVERS

1 tablespoon fennel seeds, crushed	3 tablespoons brandy or low-sodium chicken broth
1 tablespoon grated lemon zest	1 teaspoon butter
1 teaspoon olive oil	2 Granny Smith apples, cut into ¾-inch wedges
½ teaspoon salt	
3 (1¼-pound) Cornish game hens, skinned	1 onion, cut into ¾-inch wedges
⅔ cup apple cider	½ cup pitted dried plums

1 Preheat the oven to 400°F. Spray a large roasting pan with nonstick spray.

2 Mix the fennel, lemon zest, oil, and salt in a small bowl. Tie the legs of each hen together with kitchen string and rub evenly with the fennel mixture. Place the hens, breast side up, in the prepared roasting pan. Roast 30 minutes.

3 Meanwhile, bring the cider, brandy, and butter to a boil in a small saucepan. Boil 1 minute and reserve.

4 Remove the roasting pan from the oven. Spoon the apples, onion, and dried plums around the hens. Pour the cider mixture over the hens and roast, basting the hens every 15 minutes, until an instant-read thermometer inserted into a thigh registers 165°F, 30 minutes.

5 Transfer 1 of the hens to a container and let cool. Cover and refrigerate up to 3 days for later use in Caribbean Cornish Hen and Sweet Potato Salad, opposite. Cut the remaining 2 hens in half. Place the hen halves and apple mixture on a platter. Serve with the sauce from the pan, skimmed of any visible fat.

PER SERVING (½ hen with ¾ cup apple mixture and 2½ tablespoons sauce): 313 Cal, 7 g Fat, 2 g Sat Fat, 0 g Trans Fat, 134 mg Chol, 282 mg Sod, 30 g Carb, 4 g Fib, 30 g Prot, 51 mg Calc. **POINTS** value: **6.**

Caribbean Cornish Hen and Sweet Potato Salad

prep 10 MIN • cook 20 MIN • serves 4

2   sweet potatoes, peeled and cubed
1   reserved cooked Cornish hen from Cornish Hens with Apples (opposite)
1   (5½-ounce) can pineapple chunks, drained
1   red bell pepper, diced
2   scallions, thinly sliced
3   tablespoons low-fat raspberry vinaigrette

1 Bring the potatoes and enough lightly salted water to cover to a boil in a large saucepan. Reduce the heat and simmer until the potatoes are fork-tender, 12–15 minutes. Drain and transfer to a large bowl and let cool 10 minutes.

2 Meanwhile, remove the meat from the bones of the hen and chop.

3 Add the hen, pineapple, bell pepper, and scallions to the potatoes; mix well. Add the vinaigrette and toss gently to coat.

PER SERVING (1¼ cups): 211 Cal, 5 g Fat, 1 g Sat Fat, 0 g Trans Fat, 67 mg Chol, 318 mg Sod, 24 g Carb, 3 g Fib, 16 g Prot, 49 mg Calc.
POINTS value: **4.**

make this... # Duck with Brandied Cherries

prep 10 MIN • cook 15 MIN • serves 4 PLUS LEFTOVERS

6	(5-ounce) boneless skinless duck breasts
½	teaspoon salt
½	cup orange juice
3	tablespoons brandy or orange juice
1	tablespoon reduced-sodium soy sauce

1½	teaspoons sugar
1	teaspoon cornstarch
1	(10-ounce) bag frozen pitted cherries, thawed
1	teaspoon butter

1 Sprinkle the duck breasts with the salt. Spray a large nonstick skillet with nonstick spray and set over medium-high heat. Add the duck breasts and cook until cooked through, 4 minutes on each side. Transfer 2 of the duck breasts to a container and let cool. Cover and refrigerate up to 3 days for later use in Savory Duck and Corn Salad, opposite. Transfer the remaining 4 duck breasts to a cutting board, cover loosely with foil, and keep warm.

2 To make the sauce, whisk the orange juice, brandy, soy sauce, sugar, and cornstarch in a small bowl until smooth. Add the juice mixture and the cherries to the skillet; bring to a boil. Reduce the heat and simmer, stirring occasionally, until the sauce thickens slightly, 3–4 minutes. Stir in the butter. Cut 4 duck breasts into ½-inch-thick slices and serve with the sauce.

PER SERVING (1 duck breast with generous ⅓ cup sauce): 236 Cal, 2 g Fat, 1 g Sat Fat, 0 g Trans Fat, 85 mg Chol, 389 mg Sod, 17 g Carb, 2 g Fib, 30 g Prot, 27 mg Calc. **POINTS** value: **4.**

Savory Duck and Corn Salad

prep 10 MIN • cook NONE • serves 4

2	reserved cooked duck breasts from Duck with Brandied Cherries (opposite), chopped
3	cups frozen corn kernels, thawed
1	cup grape tomatoes, halved
½	red onion, thinly sliced

12	pitted kalamata olives, chopped
¼	cup chopped fresh basil
1	tablespoon cider vinegar
1	teaspoon olive oil
¼	teaspoon salt

Mix all the ingredients in a large bowl.

PER SERVING (generous 1 cup): 202 Cal, 4 g Fat, 1 g Sat Fat, 0 g Trans Fat, 41 mg Chol, 382 mg Sod, 27 g Carb, 4 g Fib, 18 g Prot, 34 mg Calc. *POINTS* value: *4.*

◆ Filling Extra

Spoon each serving of the salad into lettuce cups and sprinkle with chopped fresh chives.

make this...

Grilled Duck with Spicy Grapefruit Salsa

prep 15 MIN • grill 15 MIN • serves 4 PLUS LEFTOVERS

1 tablespoon five-spice powder	**½** red onion, minced
2 teaspoons olive oil	**2** tablespoons chopped fresh cilantro
¾ teaspoon salt	**1** jalapeño pepper, seeded and minced
6 whole duck legs, skinned	**1** tablespoon cider vinegar
1 grapefruit, peeled and cut into sections	**2** teaspoons honey
3 plum tomatoes, diced	

1 Spray the grill rack with nonstick spray and prepare a medium fire.

2 Mix the five-spice powder, 1 teaspoon of the oil, and ½ teaspoon of the salt in a small bowl. Rub the mixture all over the duck legs. Place the duck legs on the grill rack and grill, turning, until cooked through, 15 minutes.

3 Meanwhile, to make the salsa, mix the grapefruit, tomatoes, onion, cilantro, jalapeño, vinegar, honey, and the remaining 1 teaspoon of oil and ¼ teaspoon of salt in a medium bowl.

4 Transfer 2 of the duck legs to a container and let cool. Cover and refrigerate up to 3 days for later use in Duck Hash, opposite. Serve the remaining 4 duck legs with the salsa.

PER SERVING (1 duck leg and ½ cup salsa): 247 Cal, 7 g Fat, 2 g Sat Fat, 0 g Trans Fat, 127 mg Chol, 435 mg Sod, 12 g Carb, 2 g Fib, 34 g Prot, 60 mg Calc. **POINTS** value: **5.**

Duck Hash

prep 10 MIN • cook 20 MIN • serves 4

2	teaspoons olive oil		2	cups refrigerated ready-to-cook diced potatoes
1	onion, diced		½	teaspoon salt
1	green bell pepper, diced		4	large eggs
2	reserved whole cooked duck legs from Grilled Duck with Spicy Grapefruit Salsa (opposite)		½	cup shredded low-fat cheddar cheese

1 Heat the oil in a large skillet over medium-high heat. Add the onion and bell pepper; cook, stirring occasionally, until tender, 6 minutes.

2 Meanwhile, remove the meat from the bones of the duck legs and chop.

3 Stir the duck, potatoes, and salt into the onion mixture. Reduce the heat and cook, stirring occasionally, until the potatoes begin to brown, 6–8 minutes. Break the eggs over the top; cover and cook just until the eggs are set, 5–7 minutes. Sprinkle the cheese over the eggs. Cover and cook until the cheese melts, 2–3 minutes.

PER SERVING (generous ½ cup hash with 1 egg): 303 Cal, 12 g Fat, 4 g Sat Fat, 0 g Trans Fat, 279 mg Chol, 714 mg Sod, 20 g Carb, 3 g Fib, 28 g Prot, 163 mg Calc. **POINTS** value: **6.**

chapter 3
Pasta! Pasta!

Hoisin Noodles with Beef and Broccoli 94
Beef-Noodle Soup Bowl 95

Tex-Mex Chili Pasta 96
Spicy Taco Soup 97

Chinese Pork and Noodles 98
Thai Coconut Soup 99

Braised Chicken and Couscous 100
Chicken-Couscous Salad 101

Chicken Mac 'n' Cheese 102
Mac 'n' Cheese Cakes with Greens and Ham 103

Ravioli Bolognese 104
Ravioli Minestrone 105

Baked Pasta and Meatballs 106
Sicilian Meatball Soup 107

Spaghetti Primavera with Sausage 108
Spaghetti and Spinach Frittata 109

Penne with Sausage and Broccoli 110
Tuscan Pasta and Bean Salad with Tuna 111

Rotini with Shrimp and Corn 112
Baked Pasta e Fagioli 113

Linguine with Asparagus and Ricotta 114
Pasta "Pizza" 115

Roasted Vegetable–Feta Pasta 116
Greek Vegetable-Noodle Soup 117

Hoisin Noodles with Beef and Broccoli

prep 20 MIN • cook 20 MIN • serves 4 PLUS LEFTOVERS

5 cups small broccoli florets	1½ teaspoons Asian chili-garlic sauce
½ pound soba noodles	1 teaspoon cornstarch
1 (1½-pound) flank steak, trimmed	1 red bell pepper, thinly sliced
3 tablespoons hoisin sauce	1 onion, thinly sliced
Juice of 1 lime	1 tablespoon minced peeled fresh ginger

1 Bring a large pot of water to a boil. Add the broccoli and cook until crisp-tender, 2 minutes. Remove with a slotted spoon to a plate. Return the water to a boil and cook the soba noodles according to the package directions.

2 Meanwhile, cut the steak in half lengthwise. Cut crosswise into ¼-inch slices. Mix the hoisin sauce, lime juice, chili-garlic sauce, and cornstarch in a small bowl until smooth.

3 Spray a large nonstick skillet with nonstick spray and set over medium-high heat. Add one-third of the beef and cook, stirring constantly, just until browned, 1–2 minutes. Transfer to a plate. Repeat with the remaining beef.

4 Add the bell pepper and onion to the skillet. Reduce the heat and cook, stirring constantly, until crisp-tender, 5 minutes. Add the ginger and cook, stirring constantly, until fragrant, 1 minute. Add the hoisin sauce mixture and cook, stirring frequently, until the sauce simmers, 1 minute. Add the beef and broccoli; cook, stirring frequently, until heated through, 2 minutes.

5 Drain the noodles. Rinse under cold running water until cool and drain. Transfer 1½ cups of the beef mixture and 2 cups of the noodles into separate containers and let cool. Cover and refrigerate up to 3 days for later use in Beef-Noodle Soup Bowl, opposite. Add the remaining 2 cups of noodles to the skillet and cook until heated through, 1 minute.

PER SERVING (2 cups): 361 Cal, 6 g Fat, 2 g Sat Fat, 0 g Trans Fat, 83 mg Chol, 539 mg Sod, 38 g Carb, 7 g Fib, 40 g Prot, 64 mg Calc. **POINTS** value: **7.**

Beef-Noodle Soup Bowl

prep 10 MIN · cook 15 MIN · serves 4

1   (32-ounce) carton low-sodium chicken broth
1   (8-ounce) package sliced fresh mushrooms
3   small carrots, thinly sliced
2   teaspoons minced peeled fresh ginger
1   garlic clove, minced
¼   teaspoon salt

1½ cups reserved cooked beef mixture and 2 cups reserved cooked noodles from Hoisin Noodles with Beef and Broccoli (opposite)
1   bunch watercress, trimmed
3   scallions, sliced
1   teaspoon Asian (dark) sesame oil

1 Bring the broth, mushrooms, carrots, ginger, garlic, and salt to a boil in a Dutch oven. Reduce the heat; cover and simmer until the mushrooms are tender, 5 minutes.

2 Meanwhile, cut the beef into bite-size pieces.

3 Add the beef, noodles, watercress, and scallions to the Dutch oven. Cover and cook until the soup is hot, 2 minutes. Stir in the oil.

PER SERVING (1½ cups): 266 Cal, 6 g Fat, 1 g Sat Fat, 0 g Trans Fat, 41 mg Chol, 367 mg Sod, 30 g Carb, 4 g Fib, 28 g Prot, 61 mg Calc. **POINTS** value: **5.**

In the Kitchen

If you don't have soba noodles or don't like the flavor of buckwheat, substitute ½ pound whole-wheat capellini pasta.

Tex-Mex Chili Pasta

prep 10 MIN • cook 20 MIN • serves 6 PLUS LEFTOVERS

- ¾ **pound whole-wheat fusilli**
- 1 **onion, chopped**
- 1 **green bell pepper, chopped**
- 1¼ **pounds lean ground beef (5% fat or less)**
- 2 **tablespoons chili powder**
- 1½ **teaspoons ground cumin**

- ½ **teaspoon salt**
- 1 **(14½-ounce) can stewed tomatoes**
- 1 **(15½-ounce) can black beans, rinsed and drained**
- 1½ **cups low-sodium tomato-vegetable juice**
- ½ **cup shredded low-fat Mexican cheese blend**

1 Cook the fusilli according to the package directions, omitting the salt if desired.

2 Meanwhile spray a 12-inch deep nonstick skillet with nonstick spray and set over medium heat. Add the onion and bell pepper; cook, stirring occasionally, until softened, 5 minutes. Increase the heat to medium-high; add the beef and brown, breaking it apart with a wooden spoon. Add the chili powder, cumin, and salt; cook, stirring constantly, until fragrant, 1 minute. Stir in the tomatoes, beans, and vegetable juice; bring to a boil. Reduce the heat and simmer, stirring occasionally, until the flavors are blended, 5 minutes.

3 Stir in the fusilli. Transfer 4 cups of the pasta mixture to a container and let cool. Cover and refrigerate up to 3 days for later use in Spicy Taco Soup, opposite. Serve the remaining 8 cups of pasta mixture sprinkled with the cheese.

PER SERVING (1⅓ cups with 4 teaspoons cheese): 317 Cal, 5 g Fat, 2 g Sat Fat, 0 g Trans Fat, 38 mg Chol, 670 mg Sod, 44 g Carb, 8 g Fib, 24 g Prot, 108 mg Calc. **POINTS** value: **6.**

...then this! Spicy Taco Soup

prep 5 MIN • cook 20 MIN • serves 4

1	(32-ounce) carton low-sodium chicken broth	4	cups reserved cooked Tex-Mex Chili Pasta (opposite)
1	(14¼-ounce) can diced tomatoes with green chiles	3	cups shredded lettuce
1	(10-ounce) box frozen corn kernels	8	baked tortilla chips, crumbled
3	scallions, sliced	¼	cup shredded low-fat Mexican cheese blend

1 Bring the broth, tomatoes, corn, and scallions to a boil in a Dutch oven. Reduce the heat; cover and simmer 10 minutes. Stir in the pasta and return to a boil.

2 Divide the soup among 4 bowls. Top evenly with the lettuce, tortilla chips, and cheese.

PER SERVING (2¼ cups soup with ¾ cup lettuce, 2 tortilla chips, and 1 tablespoon cheese): 370 Cal, 6 g Fat, 2 g Sat Fat, 0 g Trans Fat, 28 mg Chol, 711 mg Sod, 59 g Carb, 10 g Fib, 26 g Prot, 139 mg Calc. *POINTS* value: **7.**

◆ Filling Extra

In addition to the lettuce, tortilla chips, and cheese, sprinkle the soup with 2 diced plum tomatoes.

make this... # Chinese Pork and Noodles

prep 25 MIN • cook 20 MIN • serves 4 PLUS LEFTOVERS

½	pound rice noodles	1	red bell pepper, diced
1½	pounds pork tenderloin	4	cups coleslaw mix
⅓	cup low-sodium soy sauce	2	celery stalks, thinly sliced
2	tablespoons hoisin sauce	1	(8-ounce) can sliced water chestnuts, rinsed and drained
2	teaspoons grated peeled fresh ginger		
¼	teaspoon red pepper flakes	3	garlic cloves, minced
1	(8-ounce) package sliced fresh mushrooms	4	scallions, sliced

1 Cook the noodles according to the package directions.

2 Meanwhile, cut the pork in half lengthwise. Cut crosswise into ¼-inch slices. Mix the soy sauce, hoisin sauce, ginger, and pepper flakes in a small bowl.

3 Spray a large nonstick skillet with nonstick spray and set over medium-high heat. Add half of the pork and cook, stirring frequently, until no longer pink, 2 minutes. Transfer to a plate. Repeat with the remaining pork.

4 Transfer 1 cup of the noodles and 1½ cups of the pork to separate containers for later use in Thai Coconut Soup, opposite. Reserve the remaining 2½ cups of pork and 3 cups of noodles.

5 Spray the skillet with nonstick spray and set over medium-high heat. Add the mushrooms and bell pepper; cook, stirring frequently, until the vegetables are crisp-tender, 3 minutes. Add the coleslaw mix, celery, and water chestnuts; cook, stirring frequently, until the coleslaw mix is wilted, 1 minute. Stir in the soy sauce mixture and bring to a boil. Transfer 1 cup of the vegetables to the container with the pork and let cool. Cover and refrigerate up to 3 days.

6 Add the reserved pork and garlic to the skillet; cook, stirring frequently, until fragrant, 1 minute. Add the reserved noodles and scallions; cook, tossing with tongs, until the noodles are hot, 1 minute.

PER SERVING (1¾ cups): 383 Cal, 5 g Fat, 2 g Sat Fat, 0 g Trans Fat, 68 mg Chol, 897 mg Sod, 54 g Carb, 6 g Fib, 30 g Prot, 70 mg Calc. **POINTS** value: **7.**

Thai Coconut Soup

prep 5 MIN · cook 10 MIN · serves 4

2	cups low-sodium chicken broth
1	tablespoon packed brown sugar
¾	teaspoon salt
½	teaspoon curry powder
1	tomato, diced
1½	cups reserved cooked pork, 1 cup reserved cooked vegetables, and 1 cup reserved cooked noodles from Chinese Pork and Noodles (opposite)

4	ounces snow peas, trimmed and halved
1	cup light (low-fat) coconut milk
	Juice of ½ lime
¼	cup packed fresh cilantro leaves or small basil leaves

1 Bring the broth, brown sugar, salt, and curry powder to a boil in a large saucepan. Stir in the tomato, pork, and vegetables; return to a boil. Stir in the snow peas and cook until crisp-tender, about 1 minute. Stir in the coconut milk and noodles. Reduce the heat and cook, stirring occasionally, until the noodles are hot, 1 minute.

2 Remove the pan from the heat. Stir in the lime juice and cilantro.

PER SERVING (1⅓ cups): 200 Cal, 5 g Fat, 3 g Sat Fat, 0 g Trans Fat, 22 mg Chol, 724 mg Sod, 26 g Carb, 3 g Fib, 14 g Prot, 39 mg Calc. *POINTS* value: *4.*

Braised Chicken and Couscous

prep 10 MIN • cook 35 MIN • serves 4 PLUS LEFTOVERS

2	cups Israeli couscous	¼	teaspoon ground ginger
6	(5-ounce) boneless skinless chicken thighs, trimmed	¼	teaspoon black pepper
½	teaspoon salt	⅛	teaspoon cayenne
1	onion, chopped	½	cup low-sodium chicken broth
2	garlic cloves, minced	1	(14½-ounce) can diced tomatoes
¼	teaspoon cinnamon	1	tablespoon honey
		1	large zucchini, cut into ¾-inch chunks

1 Cook the couscous according to the package directions.

2 Meanwhile, sprinkle the chicken with ¼ teaspoon of the salt. Spray a large skillet with nonstick spray and set over medium-high heat. Add the chicken and cook until browned, about 4 minutes on each side. Transfer to a plate.

3 Add the onion to the skillet; reduce the heat and cook, stirring occasionally, until softened, 5 minutes. Add the garlic, cinnamon, ginger, black pepper, cayenne, and the remaining ¼ teaspoon of salt; cook, stirring constantly, until fragrant, 1 minute. Add the broth, tomatoes, and honey; bring to a boil, stirring to scrape up any brown bits from the bottom of the skillet. Stir in the chicken. Reduce the heat; cover and simmer 10 minutes. Turn the chicken and stir in the zucchini. Cover and cook, stirring occasionally, until the chicken is cooked through and the zucchini is tender, 10 minutes.

4 Fluff the couscous with a fork. Transfer 2 of the chicken thighs and 2 cups of the couscous to separate containers and let cool. Cover and refrigerate up to 2 days for later use in Chicken-Couscous Salad, opposite. Serve the remaining 4 chicken thighs and 2 cups of couscous with the sauce.

PER SERVING (1 chicken thigh with ½ cup couscous and ¾ cup sauce): 396 Cal, 12 g Fat, 4 g Sat Fat, 0 g Trans Fat, 88 mg Chol, 644 mg Sod, 36 g Carb, 4 g Fib, 36 g Prot, 98 mg Calc. *POINTS* value: *8.*

Chicken-Couscous Salad

prep 15 MIN • cook NONE • serves 4

Juice of ½ lemon

2 teaspoons olive oil

½ teaspoon salt

⅛ teaspoon ground cumin

2 reserved cooked chicken thighs and 2 cups reserved cooked couscous from Braised Chicken and Couscous (opposite)

1 (15-ounce) can chickpeas, rinsed and drained

1 small cucumber, peeled, seeded, and thinly sliced

1 large tomato, diced

¼ cup pimiento-stuffed green olives, chopped

2 tablespoons chopped fresh mint

4 cups baby spinach

1 To make the dressing, whisk the lemon juice, oil, salt, and cumin in a large bowl until blended.

2 Shred the chicken. Add the chicken, couscous, chickpeas, cucumber, tomato, olives, and mint to the dressing; toss well. Let stand until the flavors are blended, 10 minutes. Serve over the spinach.

PER SERVING (1½ cups salad with 1 cup spinach): 394 Cal, 12 g Fat, 3 g Sat Fat, 0 g Trans Fat, 44 mg Chol, 929 mg Sod, 46 g Carb, 8 g Fib, 27 g Prot, 110 mg Calc. *POINTS* value: **8.**

◆ Filling Extra

For additional crunch, add a diced red or yellow bell pepper before tossing the salad with the dressing in step 2.

make this... Chicken Mac 'n' Cheese

prep 15 MIN • cook/bake 45 MIN • serves 4 PLUS LEFTOVERS

¾   **pound whole-wheat elbow macaroni**

1   **pound ground skinless chicken breast**

2   **tablespoons all-purpose flour**

1   **(12-ounce) can evaporated fat-free milk**

1   **(8-ounce) bag shredded low-fat Mexican cheese blend**

1   **cup frozen corn kernels, thawed**

¾   **cup salsa**

1   **(4-ounce) can diced green chiles**

4   **scallions, chopped**

½   **teaspoon salt**

1   **small zucchini, shredded**

2   **plum tomatoes, thinly sliced**

1 Preheat the oven to 375°F. Line an 8-inch square baking pan with plastic wrap. Spray the plastic wrap with nonstick spray. Spray a 2½-quart shallow baking dish with nonstick spray.

2 Cook the macaroni according to the package directions, omitting the salt if desired.

3 Meanwhile, set a large nonstick skillet over medium-high heat. Add the chicken and cook, stirring to break it apart with a wooden spoon, until no longer pink, 5 minutes. Stir in the flour; reduce the heat and cook, stirring constantly, 1 minute. Gradually stir in the milk until blended. Cook, stirring occasionally, until thickened, 2 minutes.

4 Drain the macaroni in a colander, then rinse under cold running water; drain again. Return the macaroni to the pasta pot. Add the chicken mixture, cheese, corn, salsa, chiles, scallions, and salt, stirring until the cheese melts. Spread half the pasta mixture (5½ cups) in the prepared baking pan and let cool. Cover and refrigerate up to 2 days for later use in Mac 'n' Cheese Cakes with Greens and Ham, opposite.

5 Stir the zucchini into the remaining pasta mixture and transfer to the prepared baking dish; top with the tomatoes. Bake until hot and browned at the edges, 25 minutes. Let stand 5 minutes before serving.

PER SERVING (1¾ cups): 345 Cal, 5 g Fat, 2 g Sat Fat, 0 g Trans Fat, 42 mg Chol, 793 mg Sod, 46 g Carb, 5 g Fib, 32 g Prot, 274 mg Calc. **POINTS** value: **7.**

Mac 'n' Cheese Cakes with Greens and Ham

prep 15 MIN • cook 50 MIN • serves 6

1	pound kale, stems removed and torn into large pieces
1	small onion, thinly sliced
2	ounces baked ham, cut into thin strips
1	garlic clove, minced
¼	teaspoon red pepper flakes

¼	teaspoon salt
5½	cups reserved cooked pasta mixture from Chicken Mac 'n' Cheese (opposite)
¼	cup cornmeal
2	teaspoons olive oil

1 Bring a pot of lightly salted water to a boil. Add the kale and cook until crisp-tender, 8 minutes. Drain, reserving ½ cup of the cooking liquid.

2 Spray the pot with nonstick spray and set over medium heat. Add the onion and cook, stirring occasionally, until softened, 5 minutes. Add the ham and cook, stirring occasionally, until lightly browned, about 3 minutes. Add the garlic, pepper flakes, and salt; cook, stirring constantly, until fragrant, 1 minute. Add the kale and the reserved ½ cup of cooking liquid; bring to a boil. Reduce the heat; partially cover and cook until the kale is tender, 10 minutes.

3 Meanwhile, to make the cakes, cut the pasta into 6 rectangles. Spread the cornmeal on a sheet of wax paper. Dip the top and bottom of each cake into the cornmeal to coat.

4 Heat the oil in a large nonstick skillet over medium heat. Add the cakes and cook until browned and heated through, about 6 minutes on each side. Serve topped with the kale mixture.

PER SERVING (1 cake with ½ cup kale mixture): 308 Cal, 6 g Fat, 2 g Sat Fat, 0 g Trans Fat, 33 mg Chol, 908 mg Sod, 41 g Carb, 5 g Fib, 25 g Prot, 243 mg Calc. *POINTS* value: *6.*

make this... Ravioli Bolognese

prep 15 MIN • cook 20 MIN • serves 4 PLUS LEFTOVERS

2   (9-ounce) packages refrigerated low-fat cheese ravioli

1¼ pounds ground skinless turkey

1   small onion, chopped

1   celery stalk, chopped

½   cup shredded carrot

1   (26-ounce) jar fat-free chunky vegetable marinara sauce

1   yellow squash, diced

1 Cook the ravioli according to the package directions.

2 Meanwhile, set a large nonstick skillet over medium-high heat. Add the turkey, onion, celery, and carrot; cook, breaking up the turkey with a wooden spoon, until no longer pink, about 6 minutes. Stir in the marinara sauce and squash; bring to a boil. Reduce the heat; partially cover and simmer until the squash is tender, 12 minutes.

3 Transfer 1½ cups of the ravioli and 2 cups of the bolognese sauce to separate containers and let cool. Cover and refrigerate up to 3 days for later use in Ravioli Minestrone, opposite. Stir the remaining 2½ cups of ravioli into the remaining 4 cups of bolognese sauce until combined.

PER SERVING (generous 1½ cups): 385 Cal, 9 g Fat, 3 g Sat Fat, 0 g Trans Fat, 98 mg Chol, 928 mg Sod, 43 g Carb, 4 g Fib, 33 g Prot, 139 mg Calc. *POINTS* value: *8.*

...then this! Ravioli Minestrone

prep 5 MIN • cook 20 MIN • serves 4

3 cups low-sodium chicken broth

1 (15½-ounce) can kidney beans, rinsed
   and drained

2 cups reserved cooked sauce and 1½ cups reserved
   cooked ravioli from Ravioli Bolognese (opposite)

1 (6-ounce) bag baby spinach

1 Bring the broth, beans, and sauce to a boil in a Dutch oven. Reduce the heat; cover and simmer until the flavors are blended, 5 minutes.

2 Uncover, increase the heat, and return the broth mixture to a boil. Stir in the spinach. Cover and cook until the spinach wilts, 1 minute.

3 Stir in the ravioli and reduce the heat. Cover and simmer until the ravioli is heated through, 2 minutes.

PER SERVING (generous 1½ cups): 348 Cal, 7 g Fat, 2 g Sat Fat, 0 g Trans Fat, 52 mg Chol, 765 mg Sod, 46 g Carb, 8 g Fib, 29 g Prot, 154 mg Calc. **POINTS** value: **7.**

Baked Pasta and Meatballs

prep 35 MIN • cook/bake 40 MIN • serves 6 PLUS LEFTOVERS

¾ **pound farfalle**

1¼ **pounds ground skinless turkey**

⅓ **cup plain fat-free Greek yogurt**

¼ **cup seasoned dried bread crumbs**

¼ **cup grated pecorino cheese**

½ **teaspoon minced garlic**

¼ **teaspoon salt**

1 **(10-ounce) package frozen chopped spinach, thawed and squeezed dry**

1 **(24-ounce) jar fat-free marinara sauce**

1 **cup shredded fat-free mozzarella cheese**

1 Preheat the oven to 400°F. Spray a rimmed baking sheet and a shallow 2½-quart baking dish with nonstick spray.

2 Cook the farfalle according to the package directions, omitting the salt if desired.

3 Meanwhile, mix the turkey, yogurt, bread crumbs, pecorino, garlic, and salt in a large bowl. Form into 48 (1-inch) meatballs and place on the prepared baking sheet. Bake until cooked through, 10–12 minutes.

4 Transfer 24 of the meatballs and 2 cups of the ditalini into a container and let cool. Cover and refrigerate up to 3 days for later use in Sicilian Meatball Soup, opposite.

5 Mix the spinach, the remaining 24 meatballs and 4 cups of farfalle, the marinara sauce, and ½ cup of the mozzarella in a large bowl. Transfer to the prepared baking dish and sprinkle with the remaining ½ cup of mozzarella. Cover loosely with foil and bake 20 minutes. Uncover and bake until hot and bubbling at the edges, 10 minutes.

PER SERVING (1⅓ cups): 331 Cal, 5 g Fat, 2 g Sat Fat, 0 g Trans Fat, 37 mg Chol, 909 mg Sod, 46 g Carb, 5 g Fib, 26 g Prot, 293 mg Calc. **POINTS** value: **6.**

Sicilian Meatball Soup

prep 15 MIN • cook 30 MIN • serves 4

1	onion, chopped
3	small carrots, chopped
1	garlic clove, minced
1	(32-ounce) carton low-sodium chicken broth
1	(14½-ounce) can Italian-style diced tomatoes
3	cups coarsely chopped cauliflower
1	cup water

½	teaspoon salt
1	large zucchini, diced
24	reserved cooked meatballs and 2 cups reserved cooked farfalle from Baked Pasta and Meatballs (opposite)
¼	cup grated pecorino cheese

1 Spray a Dutch oven with nonstick spray and set over medium heat. Add the onion and cook, stirring occasionally, until softened, 5 minutes. Add the carrots and garlic; cook, stirring frequently, until fragrant, 1 minute. Stir in the broth, tomatoes, cauliflower, water, and salt; bring to a boil. Reduce the heat; cover and simmer 10 minutes.

2 Stir in the zucchini; cover and simmer until the vegetables are tender, 5 minutes. Stir in the meatballs and ditalini; cover and simmer until heated through, 5 minutes. Remove the Dutch oven from the heat and stir in the cheese until blended.

PER SERVING (2½ cups): 275 Cal, 9 g Fat, 3 g Sat Fat, 0 g Trans Fat, 55 mg Chol, 891 mg Sod, 24 g Carb, 6 g Fib, 29 g Prot, 252 mg Calc. **POINTS** value: **5.**

◆ Filling Extra

Accompany either the Baked Pasta and Meatballs or the Sicilian Meatball Soup with an easy salad made with refrigerator staples. Toss 2 peeled, seeded, and sliced cucumbers, 2 cups shredded romaine lettuce, 2 sliced scallions, juice of ½ lemon, and salt and black pepper to taste in a large bowl.

make this... Spaghetti Primavera with Sausage

prep 15 MIN • cook 25 MIN • serves 4 PLUS LEFTOVERS

¾ **pound whole-wheat spaghetti**

½ **pound fully-cooked Italian chicken sausage, cut into ¼-inch slices**

1 **teaspoon olive oil**

1 **onion, chopped**

3 **garlic cloves, thinly sliced**

1 **(10-ounce) box frozen peas and carrots**

2 **yellow squash, diced**

2 **cups cherry tomatoes, halved**

¾ **teaspoon salt**

1 **cup packed fresh basil leaves, thinly sliced**

1 Cook the spaghetti according to the package directions, omitting the salt if desired.

2 Meanwhile, spray a large nonstick skillet with nonstick spray and set over medium heat. Add the sausage and cook, stirring occasionally, until browned, about 5 minutes. Transfer to a plate.

3 Add the oil and onion to the skillet; cook, stirring occasionally, until softened, 5 minutes. Add the garlic and cook, stirring frequently, until fragrant, 1 minute. Add the peas and carrots, squash, tomatoes, and salt; cook, stirring occasionally, until the vegetables are tender, 10 minutes.

4 Drain the spaghetti, reserving ¼ cup of the cooking water. Return the spaghetti to the pasta pot; add the vegetable mixture and toss to coat. Transfer 4 cups of the pasta mixture to a container and let cool. Cover and refrigerate up to 3 days for later use in Spaghetti and Spinach Frittata, opposite.

5 Add the sausage, basil, and the reserved pasta cooking water to the remaining pasta mixture. Cook over medium heat, tossing gently, until heated through, 1 minute.

PER SERVING (about 1¾ cups): 373 Cal, 9 g Fat, 2 g Sat Fat, 0 g Trans Fat, 33 mg Chol, 917 mg Sod, 57 g Carb, 8 g Fib, 22 g Prot, 82 mg Calc. **POINTS** value: **7.**

Spaghetti and Spinach Frittata

prep 10 MIN · cook/broil 15 MIN · serves 4

5   large egg whites

4   large eggs

4   cups reserved cooked pasta mixture from
    Spaghetti Primavera with Sausage (opposite)

1   (10-ounce) package frozen chopped spinach,
    thawed and squeezed dry

½   cup shredded low-fat cheddar cheese

¼   teaspoon salt

1 Preheat the broiler.

2 Whisk the egg whites and eggs in a large bowl until blended. Stir in the pasta, spinach, ¼ cup of the cheese, and the salt until well blended.

3 Spray a 10-inch ovenproof nonstick skillet with nonstick spray and set over medium heat. Add the egg mixture and spread evenly. Cover and cook until the edges are set, 8 minutes. Place the skillet under the broiler and broil 5 inches from the heat until set in the center, 5 minutes. Sprinkle with the remaining ¼ cup of cheese and broil until the cheese melts, 1 minute. Let stand 5 minutes before cutting into 4 wedges.

PER SERVING (1 wedge): 270 Cal, 8 g Fat, 2 g Sat Fat, 0 g Trans Fat, 215 mg Chol, 729 mg Sod, 31 g Carb, 6 g Fib, 22 g Prot, 229 mg Calc. **POINTS** value: **5.**

make this... Penne with Sausage and Broccoli

prep 15 MIN • cook 30 MIN • serves 4 PLUS LEFTOVERS

½   pound whole-wheat penne

1   onion, chopped

2   garlic cloves, minced

1   pint grape tomatoes, halved

¼   teaspoon salt

⅛   teaspoon black pepper

¾   pound hot Italian turkey sausage links, casings removed

4   cups small broccoli florets

¼   cup grated pecorino cheese

1 Cook the penne according to the package directions, omitting the salt if desired.

2 Meanwhile, spray a large nonstick skillet with nonstick spray and set over medium-low heat. Add the onion and cook, stirring occasionally, until softened, 8 minutes. Add the garlic and cook, stirring frequently, until fragrant, 1 minute. Add the tomatoes, salt, and pepper; cook, stirring occasionally, until the tomatoes begin to soften, 5 minutes. Remove the skillet from the heat.

3 Drain the penne, reserving 1¼ cups of the cooking water. Add the penne to the skillet and stir to coat. Transfer 2½ cups of the pasta mixture to a container and let cool. Cover and refrigerate up to 3 days for later use in Tuscan Pasta and Bean Salad with Tuna, opposite. Transfer the remaining 4½ cups of pasta mixture to a large bowl and reserve.

4 Wipe the skillet clean and set over medium heat. Add the sausage and cook, stirring to break it apart with a wooden spoon, until browned about 6 minutes. Add the broccoli and 1 cup of the reserved pasta cooking water; bring to a boil. Reduce the heat; cover and cook until the broccoli is tender, 3–4 minutes. Add the reserved 4½ cups of pasta mixture to the skillet and cook, stirring occasionally, until the pasta is heated through, 2 minutes. (If the mixture seems dry add the remaining ¼ cup of reserved cooking liquid.) Remove the skillet from the heat and stir in the cheese.

PER SERVING (2 cups): 364 Cal, 12 g Fat, 3 g Sat Fat, 0 g Trans Fat, 83 mg Chol, 994 mg Sod, 36 g Carb, 6 g Fib, 31 g Prot, 164 mg Calc. **POINTS** value: **7.**

...then this! Tuscan Pasta and Bean Salad with Tuna

prep 15 MIN • microwave 5 MIN • serves 4

1 (9-ounce) box frozen cut green beans

Juice of ½ lemon

2 teaspoons olive oil

½ teaspoon salt

1 (15½-ounce) can cannellini beans, rinsed and drained

1 (6-ounce) can solid-white tuna packed in water, drained and broken into chunks

½ small red onion, thinly sliced

6 kalamata olives, pitted and chopped

2½ cups reserved cooked pasta mixture from Penne with Sausage and Broccoli (opposite)

1 Microwave the green beans according to the package directions and drain.

2 Meanwhile, whisk the lemon juice, oil, and salt in a large bowl until blended.

3 Stir in the green beans, cannellini beans, tuna, onion, olives, and pasta mixture; toss to coat. Let stand until the flavors are blended, 15 minutes.

PER SERVING (generous 1½ cups): 276 Cal, 4 g Fat, 1 g Sat Fat, 0 g Trans Fat, 12 mg Chol, 836 mg Sod, 41 g Carb, 9 g Fib, 22 g Prot, 118 mg Calc. **POINTS** value: **5.**

make this... Rotini with Shrimp and Corn

prep 20 MIN • cook 20 MIN • serves 4 PLUS LEFTOVERS

¾	**pound whole-wheat rotini**
4	**ears corn on the cob, kernels removed**
3	**teaspoons olive oil**
3	**garlic cloves, slivered**
3	**large tomatoes, diced**

¾	**teaspoon salt**
¼	**teaspoon black pepper**
½	**cup packed fresh basil leaves, coarsely chopped**
1	**pound large shrimp, peeled and deveined**

1 Cook the rotini according to the package directions, omitting the salt if desired and adding the corn for the last 3 minutes of the cooking time.

2 Meanwhile, heat 1½ teaspoons of the oil in a large skillet over medium heat. Add the garlic and cook, stirring frequently, until lightly golden, about 2 minutes. Add the tomatoes, ½ teaspoon of the salt, and the pepper; bring just to a boil. Reduce the heat and simmer, stirring occasionally, until the tomatoes begin to soften and release their juice, 3 minutes. Stir in the basil.

3 Drain the rotini and the corn, reserving ¼ cup of the cooking water. Return the rotini and corn to the pasta pot; stir in the tomato mixture. Transfer half of the pasta mixture (4 cups) to a container and let cool. Cover and refrigerate up to 3 days for later use in Baked Pasta e Fagioli, opposite. Cover the pasta pot and keep the remaining 4 cups of pasta mixture warm.

4 Wipe the skillet clean. Sprinkle the shrimp with the remaining ¼ teaspoon of salt. Heat the remaining 1½ teaspoons of oil in the skillet over medium-high heat. Add the shrimp and cook just until pink, about 1 minute on each side. Add the reserved pasta cooking water and bring to a boil. Transfer the shrimp mixture to the pasta pot and mix well.

PER SERVING (1½ cups): 296 Cal, 5 g Fat, 1 g Sat Fat, 0 g Trans Fat, 107 mg Chol, 610 mg Sod, 44 g Carb, 6 g Fib, 21 g Prot, 44 mg Calc. **POINTS** value: **6.**

Baked Pasta e Fagioli

prep 10 MIN • cook/bake 35 MIN • serves 4

1	small onion, chopped
1	celery stalk, chopped
1	carrot, chopped
1	(15-ounce) can white beans, rinsed and drained
1	(8-ounce) can Italian-style tomato sauce

1	cup vegetable broth
4	cups reserved cooked pasta mixture from Rotini with Shrimp and Corn (opposite)
2	tablespoons grated Asiago cheese

1 Preheat the oven to 400°F. Spray a 2½-quart baking dish with nonstick spray.

2 Spray a large nonstick skillet with nonstick spray and set over medium-low heat. Add the onion, celery, and carrot; cover and cook, stirring occasionally, until tender, 8 minutes. Stir in the beans, tomato sauce, and broth; bring to a boil. Reduce the heat and simmer, uncovered, stirring occasionally, until the flavors are blended, 2 minutes.

3 Stir in the pasta mixture. Transfer to the prepared baking dish and sprinkle with the cheese. Cover loosely with foil and bake until hot and bubbling at the edges, 25–30 minutes.

PER SERVING (scant 1¾ cups): 390 Cal, 6 g Fat, 2 g Sat Fat, 0 g Trans Fat, 4 mg Chol, 1,151 mg Sod, 70 g Carb, 12 g Fib, 19 g Prot, 135 mg Calc. *POINTS* value: *8.*

◆ Filling Extra

Want more veggies? Shred a zucchini and cook it with the onion, celery, and carrot in step 2.

make this... # Linguine with Asparagus and Ricotta

prep 20 MIN • cook 35 MIN • serves 4 PLUS LEFTOVERS

¾ **pound whole-wheat linguine**	2 **shallots, chopped**
4 **tablespoons grated pecorino cheese**	3 **teaspoons olive oil**
	½ **teaspoon salt**
2 **tablespoons chopped fresh flat-leaf parsley**	3 **garlic cloves, minced**
1 **pound asparagus, trimmed and cut into 1½-inch pieces**	2 **(8-ounce) packages sliced fresh cremini mushrooms**
	¼ **teaspoon black pepper**
	¼ **cup part-skim ricotta cheese**

1 Preheat the oven to 425°F. Spray a 9 x 13-inch baking pan with nonstick spray.

2 Cook the linguine according to the package directions, omitting the salt if desired.

3 Meanwhile mix 2 tablespoons of the pecorino and the parsley in a cup and reserve. Toss the asparagus, shallots, 1½ teaspoons of the oil, and ¼ teaspoon of the salt in the prepared baking pan. Roast until the asparagus are tender, 15 minutes, stirring once halfway through cooking.

4 Drain the linguine, reserving ¾ cup of the cooking water. Heat the remaining 1½ teaspoons of oil in the pasta pot over medium heat. Add the garlic and cook, stirring frequently, just until golden, about 1 minute. Add the mushrooms, pepper, and the remaining ¼ teaspoon of salt; cook, stirring occasionally, until the mushrooms are tender, 10 minutes. Stir in the linguine. Transfer 4 cups of the linguine mixture to a container and let cool. Cover and refrigerate up to 3 days for later use in Pasta "Pizza," opposite.

5 Add the asparagus mixture and ½ cup of the reserved pasta cooking water to the remaining linguine mixture in the pasta pot. Set the pot over medium heat and cook, stirring frequently, until the linguine is hot, 2 minutes. (If the mixture seems dry, add the remaining ¼ cup of reserved pasta cooking water.) Remove the pot from the heat. Add the ricotta and the remaining 2 tablespoons of pecorino; mix well. Sprinkle with the reserved pecorino-parsley mixture.

PER SERVING (1½ cups): 265 Cal, 7 g Fat, 2 g Sat Fat, 0 g Trans Fat, 10 mg Chol, 551 mg Sod, 41 g Carb, 6 g Fib, 14 g Prot, 171 mg Calc. **POINTS** value: **5.**

...then this! Pasta "Pizza"

prep 15 MIN • cook/bake 40 MIN • serves 4

2   large eggs
¼   cup grated pecorino cheese
4   cups reserved cooked pasta mixture from
    Linguine with Asparagus and Ricotta (opposite)
1   onion, chopped

1   red bell pepper, coarsely chopped
1½ cups fat-free marinara sauce
½   cup low-fat sliced pepperoni, coarsely chopped
1   cup shredded fat-free mozzarella cheese

1 Preheat the oven to 375°F. Spray a 9-inch pie plate with nonstick spray. Whisk the eggs and pecorino in a large bowl until blended. Stir in the pasta mixture. Transfer to the prepared pie plate; press with the back of a spoon along the bottom and sides of the plate to form a crust.

2 Spray a large nonstick skillet with nonstick spray and set over medium heat. Add the onion and bell pepper; cook, stirring occasionally, until tender, 8 minutes. Stir in the marinara sauce and pepperoni and cook until the sauce thickens, 5 minutes; spread over the crust. Bake until heated through, 25 minutes. Sprinkle with the mozzarella and bake, 2 minutes. Let stand 5 minutes before cutting into 4 wedges.

PER SERVING (1 wedge): 377 Cal, 10 g Fat, 4 g Sat Fat, 0 g Trans Fat, 128 mg Chol, 1,246 mg Sod, 49 g Carb, 6 g Fib, 27 g Prot, 407 mg Calc. **POINTS** value: **8.**

make this... ## Roasted Vegetable–Feta Pasta

prep 15 MIN • cook/roast 20 MIN • serves 4 PLUS LEFTOVERS

1	(9-ounce) package fresh fettuccine
1½	pounds plum tomatoes, cut into 1-inch chunks
2	large zucchini, cut into ¾-inch chunks
1	yellow bell pepper, diced
1	red onion, coarsely chopped
4	garlic cloves, minced

2	teaspoons olive oil
½	teaspoon salt
¼	teaspoon black pepper
⅓	cup crumbled low-fat feta cheese with basil and tomato

1 Preheat the oven to 450°F.

2 Cook the fettuccine according to the package directions, omitting the salt if desired.

3 Meanwhile, toss the tomatoes, zucchini, bell pepper, onion, garlic, oil, salt, and black pepper in a large bowl. Divide and spread the vegetables on 2 large rimmed baking sheets. Roast until the vegetables are tender, 15 minutes, stirring once halfway through cooking.

4 Drain the fettuccine, reserving ⅓ cup of the cooking water. Transfer 1 cup of the fettuccine and 2 cups of the vegetables into separate containers and let cool. Cover and refrigerate up to 3 days for later use in Greek Vegetable-Noodle Soup, opposite.

5 Mix the remaining 2 cups of fettuccine, 3 cups of vegetables, the reserved pasta cooking water, and the cheese in the pasta pot.

PER SERVING (1½ cups): 200 Cal, 5 g Fat, 1 g Sat Fat, 0 g Trans Fat, 28 mg Chol, 512 mg Sod, 34 g Carb, 4 g Fib, 8 g Prot, 90 mg Calc. **POINTS** value: **4.**

Greek Vegetable-Noodle Soup

prep 10 MIN • cook 15 MIN • serves 4

1   (32-ounce) carton low-sodium chicken broth

1   (15½-ounce) can kidney beans, rinsed and drained

2   cups reserved cooked vegetables and 1 cup reserved cooked fettuccine from Roasted Vegetable-Feta Pasta (opposite)

½   teaspoon dried oregano

½   teaspoon salt

1   (6-ounce) bag baby spinach

¼   cup chopped fresh dill

¼   cup crumbled low-fat feta cheese

1 Bring the broth, beans, vegetables, oregano, and salt to a boil in a large saucepan. Reduce the heat; cover and simmer until the flavors are blended, 10 minutes. Add the spinach and cook, stirring frequently, until wilted, 2 minutes.

2 Meanwhile, cut the fettuccine into 2-inch pieces.

3 Add the fettuccine to the pan and cook, stirring occasionally, until heated through, 2 minutes. Stir in the dill. Serve sprinkled with the cheese.

PER SERVING (generous 1½ cups soup with 1 tablespoon cheese): 254 Cal, 5 g Fat, 1 g Sat Fat, 0 g Trans Fat, 15 mg Chol, 881 mg Sod, 40 g Carb, 8 g Fib, 17 g Prot, 142 mg Calc. **POINTS** value: **5.**

In the Kitchen

Change this recipe to use ingredients you have on hand. You can substitute chickpeas for the kidney beans and chopped escarole for the baby spinach.

chapter 4
Take it Slow

Italian-Style Pot Roast 120
Philly Cheese Steak Sandwiches 121

Slow-Cooker Beef Chili 122
Tex-Mex Taco Salad 123

Savory Slow-Cooker Meatloaf 124
Spaghetti and "Meatballs" 125

Asian-Style Pork Roast 126
Hunan Pork and Peppers 127

Smoky Bean and Ham Soup 128
Easy Cassoulet 129

Mexicali Pork Stew 130
Pork and Rice Burritos 131

Tropical Chicken 132
Buffalo Chicken Salad 133

Spanish Chicken and Rice 134
Salsa Chicken Wraps 135

Spicy Chicken Stew 136
Chicken Fried Rice 137

Tuscan Braised Turkey 138
Turkey Tonnato 139

BBQ Turkey 140
Turkey and Shrimp Gumbo 141

make this...
Italian-Style Pot Roast

prep 15 MIN • cook 4–5 HRS ON HIGH • serves 6 PLUS LEFTOVERS

1   (2½-pound) bottom round roast, trimmed

¾   teaspoon salt

¼   teaspoon black pepper

4   red potatoes, quartered

2   onions, halved and sliced

½   cup dry red wine or low-sodium chicken broth

5   garlic cloves, thinly sliced

1   (14½-ounce) can Italian-style stewed tomatoes

1½ teaspoons dried Italian seasoning

1   (8-ounce) package sliced fresh mushrooms

1   (9-ounce) box frozen Italian green beans, thawed

1 Sprinkle the beef with ½ teaspoon of the salt and the pepper. Spray a large nonstick skillet with nonstick spray and set over medium-high heat. Add the beef and cook, turning occasionally, until browned, 6 minutes. Transfer the beef to a 5- or 6-quart slow cooker. Place the potatoes around the beef.

2 Add the onions to the skillet and cook, stirring occasionally, until lightly browned, about 3 minutes. Add the wine and garlic; bring to a boil. Boil 1 minute. Stir in the tomatoes and Italian seasoning. Pour the mixture over the beef and potatoes. Top with the mushrooms in an even layer. Cover and cook until the beef is fork-tender, 4–5 hours on high or 8–10 hours on low.

3 Transfer one-third of the beef to a container; transfer ½ cup of the mushrooms and ½ cup of the sauce to a separate container and let cool. Cover and refrigerate up to 3 days for later use in Philly Cheese Steak Sandwiches, opposite. Cover the remaining two-thirds of the beef loosely with foil; reserve and keep warm. Transfer the potatoes to a bowl and reserve.

4 Add the beans and the remaining ¼ teaspoon of salt to the slow cooker. Cover and cook on high until the beans are crisp-tender, 15 minutes. Add the potatoes. Cover and cook on high until heated through, 5 minutes. Cut the beef across the grain into 12 slices. Serve with the sauce and vegetables.

PER SERVING (2 slices beef with about 1 cup sauce and vegetables): 349 Cal, 6 g Fat, 2 g Sat Fat, 0 g Trans Fat, 94 mg Chol, 364 mg Sod, 33 g Carb, 6 g Fib, 42 g Prot, 79 mg Calc. *POINTS* value: *7.*

Philly Cheese Steak Sandwiches

prep 5 MIN • cook/broil 10 MIN • serves 4

¾ **pound reserved cooked beef, ½ cup cooked mushrooms, and ½ cup sauce from Italian-Style Pot Roast (opposite)**

1 **green bell pepper, thinly sliced**

1 **onion, thinly sliced**

4 **(6-inch) French rolls, split**

4 **(¾-ounce) slices fat-free cheddar cheese**

1 Preheat the broiler.

2 Thinly slice the beef. Spray a large nonstick skillet with nonstick spray and set over medium-high heat. Add the bell pepper and onion; cook, stirring frequently, until crisp-tender, 6 minutes. Stir in the beef, mushrooms, and sauce. Reduce the heat and cook until heated through, 2 minutes.

3 Meanwhile, place the rolls, cut side up, on a baking sheet. Broil 5 inches from the heat until lightly toasted, about 30 seconds.

4 Spoon ¾ cup of the filling onto the bottom half of each roll. Top the filling evenly with the cheese. Broil until the cheese melts, 1 minute. Top with the top halves of the rolls.

PER SERVING (1 sandwich): 389 Cal, 5 g Fat, 2 g Sat Fat, 0 g Trans Fat, 69 mg Chol, 842 mg Sod, 49 g Carb, 3 g Fib, 41 g Prot, 205 mg Calc. **POINTS** value: **8.**

Slow-Cooker Beef Chili

prep 10 MIN • cook 4–5 HRS ON HIGH • serves 4 PLUS LEFTOVERS

2 pounds bottom round roast, trimmed and cut into ¾-inch chunks	1 (1¼-ounce) package reduced-sodium taco seasoning
1 large onion, chopped	1 tablespoon chili powder
2 (15½-ounce) cans pinto beans, rinsed and drained	
2 (14½-ounce) cans diced tomatoes	
1 large yellow bell pepper, diced	

1 Spray a large nonstick skillet with nonstick spray and set over medium-high heat. Add half of the beef and cook, stirring frequently, until browned, about 4 minutes. Transfer to a 5- or 6-quart slow cooker. Repeat with the remaining beef. Add the onion to the skillet and cook, stirring occasionally, until lightly browned, about 3 minutes. Stir in the beans, tomatoes, bell pepper, taco seasoning, and chili powder.

2 Add the bean mixture to the slow cooker; stir to combine. Cover and cook until the beef is fork-tender, 4–5 hours on high or 8–10 hours on low.

3 Transfer 2 cups of the chili to a microwavable bowl and let cool. Cover and refrigerate up to 3 days for later use in Tex-Mex Taco Salad, opposite. Divide the remaining 4 cups of chili among 4 bowls.

PER SERVING (1 cup): 341 Cal, 6 g Fat, 2 g Sat Fat, 0 g Trans Fat, 84 mg Chol, 431 mg Sod, 30 g Carb, 9 g Fib, 42 g Prot, 92 mg Calc. **POINTS** value: **7.**

...then this! Tex-Mex Taco Salad

prep 10 MIN • microwave 5 MIN • serves 4

2	**cups reserved cooked Slow-Cooker Beef Chili (opposite)**
6	**cups shredded iceberg lettuce**
2	**tomatoes, diced**

¼	**cup fat-free ranch dressing**
16	**baked tortilla chips, broken into pieces**
1	**cup shredded fat-free cheddar cheese**

1 Cover the chili with plastic wrap; then prick a few holes in the plastic. Microwave on High until hot, 2 minutes, stirring once halfway through cooking.

2 Meanwhile, divide the lettuce and tomatoes among 4 plates; drizzle each plate with 1 tablespoon of the dressing.

3 Top the lettuce mixture on each plate evenly with the tortilla chips, chili, and cheese.

PER SERVING (1 salad): 312 Cal, 4 g Fat, 1 g Sat Fat, 0 g Trans Fat, 48 mg Chol, 797 mg Sod, 39 g Carb, 7 g Fib, 31 g Prot, 327 mg Calc. **POINTS** value: **6.**

◆ Filling Extra

Jazz up these salads by topping the lettuce and tomatoes on each plate with a few slices red bell pepper and thinly sliced scallions.

Savory Slow-Cooker Meatloaf

prep 20 MIN • cook 3–4 HRS ON HIGH • serves 4 PLUS LEFTOVERS

1 pound lean ground beef (5% fat or less)	1 small onion, finely chopped
1 pound ground skinless turkey	2 large eggs, lightly beaten
1 (10-ounce) package frozen chopped spinach, thawed and squeezed dry	6 tablespoons ketchup
¾ cup seasoned dried bread crumbs	1 tablespoon + 1 teaspoon Dijon mustard
½ cup shredded carrot	1 tablespoon Worcestershire sauce
	½ teaspoon salt

1 Mix the beef, turkey, spinach, bread crumbs, carrot, onion, eggs, 3 tablespoons of the ketchup, 1 tablespoon of the mustard, the Worcestershire sauce, and salt in a large bowl. Form into a 7-inch round loaf. Place the loaf in a 5- or 6-quart slow cooker.

2 Mix the remaining 3 tablespoons of ketchup and 1 teaspoon of mustard in a small bowl. Spread over the top of the loaf. Cover and cook until an instant-read thermometer inserted into the center of the loaf registers 160°F, 3–4 hours on high or 6–8 hours on low.

3 Transfer the meatloaf to a cutting board and let stand 10 minutes. Cut the meatloaf crosswise in half. Transfer one half to a container and let cool. Cover and refrigerate up to 4 days for later use in Spaghetti and "Meatballs," opposite. Cut the remaining half of meatloaf into 8 wedges.

PER SERVING (2 slices): 246 Cal, 9 g Fat, 3 g Sat Fat, 0 g Trans Fat, 123 mg Chol, 534 mg Sod, 14 g Carb, 2 g Fib, 28 g Prot, 81 mg Calc. **POINTS** value: **5.**

Spaghetti and "Meatballs"

prep 5 MIN • cook 15 MIN • serves 6

½ **pound whole-wheat angel-hair pasta**

Reserved cooked Savory Slow-Cooker Meatloaf (opposite), cut into 1-inch meatball-size cubes

2 **cups fat-free marinara sauce**

1 Cook the pasta according to the package directions, omitting the salt if desired.

2 Meanwhile, bring the meatballs and marinara sauce to a boil in a large skillet. Reduce the heat; cover and simmer, stirring occasionally, until the meatballs are hot, 10 minutes.

3 Transfer the pasta to a large bowl. Spoon the meatballs and sauce over the pasta.

PER SERVING (generous ¾ cup pasta with ⅔ cup meatballs and sauce): 327 Cal, 7 g Fat, 2 g Sat Fat, 0 g Trans Fat, 85 mg Chol, 771 mg Sod, 39 g Carb, 5 g Fib, 26 g Prot, 77 mg Calc. **POINTS** value: **6.**

In the Kitchen

If you prefer to make a meaty sauce rather than the "meatballs" for this recipe, crumble the meatloaf into the marinara sauce and simmer until heated through.

make this... Asian-Style Pork Roast

prep 10 MIN • cook 4–5 HRS ON HIGH • serves 4 PLUS LEFTOVERS

1	(2½-pound) pork loin roast, trimmed	2	tablespoons Dijon mustard
½	teaspoon salt	1	tablespoon minced peeled fresh ginger
¼	teaspoon black pepper	3	garlic cloves, minced
1	large onion, coarsely chopped	1	(1-pound) bag baby carrots
½	cup all-fruit apricot preserves	2	cups frozen broccoli-cauliflower blend, thawed
2	tablespoons low-sodium soy sauce		

1 Sprinkle the pork with the salt and pepper. Spray a large nonstick skillet with nonstick spray and set over medium-high heat. Add the pork and cook, turning occasionally, until browned, about 6 minutes. Transfer to a 5- or 6-quart slow cooker.

2 Add the onion to the skillet and cook, stirring frequently, until lightly browned, about 3 minutes. Stir in the preserves, soy sauce, mustard, ginger, and garlic; bring to a simmer. Stir in the carrots and pour over the pork. Cover and cook until the pork is fork-tender, 4–5 hours on high or 8–10 hours on low.

3 Transfer the pork to a cutting board and cover loosely with foil. Transfer the carrots to a bowl with a slotted spoon and reserve. Add the broccoli-cauliflower blend to the slow cooker. Cover and cook on high until crisp-tender, 15 minutes. Add the reserved carrots to the slow cooker. Cover and cook on high until heated through, 5 minutes.

4 Cut the pork crosswise in half. Transfer one half of the pork to a container and let cool. Cover and refrigerate up to 3 days for later use in Hunan Pork and Peppers, opposite. Cut the remaining half of pork into 8 slices; serve with the vegetables and sauce.

PER SERVING (2 slices pork with 1 cup vegetables and sauce): 421 Cal, 12 g Fat, 4 g Sat Fat, 0 g Trans Fat, 91 mg Chol, 748 mg Sod, 44 g Carb, 9 g Fib, 36 g Prot, 91 mg Calc. **POINTS** value: **9.**

Hunan Pork and Peppers

prep 10 MIN • cook 10 MIN • serves 4

½	cup fat-free stir-fry sauce	1	red onion, diced
¼	cup water	1	green bell pepper, diced
1	tablespoon red-wine vinegar	1	red bell pepper, diced
1	garlic clove, minced	1¼	pounds reserved cooked Asian-Style Pork Roast (opposite), diced
⅛	teaspoon red pepper flakes		

1 Mix the stir-fry sauce, water, vinegar, garlic, and pepper flakes in a small bowl.

2 Spray a large nonstick skillet with nonstick spray and set over medium-high heat. Add the onion and bell peppers; cook, stirring constantly, until the vegetables are crisp-tender, 4 minutes.

3 Add the pork and the sauce mixture; bring to a boil. Reduce the heat and simmer, stirring frequently, until hot, 4 minutes.

PER SERVING (1 cup): 310 Cal, 11 g Fat, 4 g Sat Fat, 0 g Trans Fat, 91 mg Chol, 556 mg Sod, 18 g Carb, 2 g Fib, 33 g Prot, 20 mg Calc. **POINTS** value: **7.**

◆ Filling Extra

Serve this hearty stir-fry with a side of quick-cooking barley (⅔ cup cooked barley for each serving will increase the **POINTS** value by **2**).

make this... Smoky Bean and Ham Soup

prep 10 MIN • cook 5–6 HRS ON HIGH • serves 4 PLUS LEFTOVERS

1	(20-ounce) bag dried 15-bean soup mix, picked over and rinsed	1	large onion, chopped
		½	pound carrots, sliced
4	cups low-sodium chicken broth	2	celery stalks, sliced
		3	garlic cloves, minced
4	cups water	1	teaspoon dried thyme
1	(10-ounce) smoked ham hock		

1 Mix all the ingredients in a 5- or 6-quart slow cooker. Cover and cook until the beans are very tender, 5–6 hours on high or 10–12 hours on low.

2 About 30 minutes before the cooking time is up, remove the ham hock to a plate and let cool. Remove the ham from the bone and chop; discard the skin and bone. Add the meat to the slow cooker.

3 Transfer 4 cups of the soup to a container and let cool. Cover and refrigerate up to 3 days for later use in Easy Cassoulet, opposite. Divide the remaining soup among 4 bowls.

PER SERVING (1¾ cups): 362 Cal, 4 g Fat, 1 g Sat Fat, 0 g Trans Fat, 7 mg Chol, 803 mg Sod, 65 g Carb, 21 g Fib, 22 g Prot, 151 mg Calc. **POINTS** value: **7.**

Easy Cassoulet

prep 5 MIN • cook 15 MIN • serves 4

¾ **pound fully-cooked chicken sausages, thickly sliced**

4 **cups reserved cooked Smoky Bean and Ham Soup (opposite)**

1 **(14½-ounce) can diced tomatoes with roasted garlic, drained**

½ **pound kale, stems removed, chopped**

1 Spray a large nonstick skillet with nonstick spray and set over medium-high heat. Add the sausages and cook, stirring occasionally, until lightly browned, about 2 minutes.

2 Add the soup, tomatoes, and kale; cover and bring to a boil. Uncover, reduce the heat, and cook, stirring frequently, until the mixture thickens slightly, 10 minutes.

PER SERVING (1¼ cups): 360 Cal, 12 g Fat, 3 g Sat Fat, 0 g Trans Fat, 53 mg Chol, 1,068 mg Sod, 39 g Carb, 12 g Fib, 27 g Prot, 114 mg Calc. **POINTS value: 7.**

Mexicali Pork Stew

prep 20 MIN • cook 5–6 HRS ON HIGH • serves 4 PLUS LEFTOVERS

1½ pounds boneless pork loin, trimmed and cut into 1½-inch chunks

¾ teaspoon salt

1 large onion, chopped

3 garlic cloves, minced

2 teaspoons chili powder

2 teaspoons ground cumin

1 teaspoon dried oregano

1 (15½-ounce) can pink beans or pinto beans, rinsed and drained

1 (14½-ounce) can petite diced tomatoes with green chiles

1 chipotle en adobo, seeded and minced + 2 teaspoons adobo sauce (without oil)

1 large zucchini, halved lengthwise and sliced

1 cup frozen corn kernels, thawed

1 Sprinkle the pork with ½ teaspoon of the salt. Spray a large nonstick skillet with nonstick spray and set over medium-high heat. Add half of the pork and cook, stirring frequently, until browned, about 6 minutes. Transfer to a 5- or 6-quart slow cooker. Repeat with the remaining pork.

2 Add the onion to the skillet and cook, stirring frequently, until browned, about 4 minutes. Add the garlic, chili powder, cumin, oregano, and the remaining ¼ teaspoon of salt; cook, stirring constantly, until fragrant, 1 minute. Stir in the beans, tomatoes, chipotle en adobo, and adobo sauce. Add the tomato mixture to the slow cooker; stir to blend. Cover and cook until the pork is fork-tender, 5–6 hours on high or 10–12 hours on low.

3 About 35 minutes before the cooking time is up, stir in the zucchini and corn. Cover and cook on high until the zucchini is tender, 30 minutes.

4 Transfer 2 cups of the stew to a microwavable bowl and let cool. Cover and refrigerate up to 3 days for later use in Pork and Rice Burritos, opposite. Divide the remaining 4 1/2 cups of stew among 4 bowls.

PER SERVING (1 generous cup): 333 Cal, 10 g Fat, 3 g Sat Fat, 0 g Trans Fat, 75 mg Chol, 637 mg Sod, 28 g Carb, 8 g Fib, 33 g Prot, 82 mg Calc. **POINTS** value: **7.**

Pork and Rice Burritos

prep 5 MIN • cook/microwave 10 MIN • serves 4

⅔ **cup instant brown rice**

2 **cups reserved cooked Mexicali Pork Stew (opposite)**

4 **(8-inch) fat-free flour tortillas**

1 **cup shredded fat-free Mexican cheese blend**

1 **cup coleslaw mix**

1 Cook the rice according to the package directions.

2 Meanwhile, cover the stew with plastic wrap; then prick a few holes in the plastic. Microwave on High until hot, 3 minutes; keep warm. Microwave the tortillas until hot according to the package directions.

3 Spoon ¼ cup of the rice and ½ cup of the stew onto each tortilla. Sprinkle evenly with the cheese and coleslaw mix. Fold two opposite sides of each tortilla over to enclose the filling.

PER SERVING (1 burrito): 357 Cal, 6 g Fat, 2 g Sat Fat, 0 g Trans Fat, 38 mg Chol, 973 mg Sod, 52 g Carb, 9 g Fib, 28 g Prot, 364 mg Calc. **POINTS** value: **7.**

◆ Filling Extra

In addition to the cheese and coleslaw, sprinkle ½ diced avocado evenly over the tortillas in step 3 (the per-serving **POINTS** value will increase by **1**).

make this... # Tropical Chicken

prep 20 MIN • cook 3–4 HRS ON HIGH • serves 4 PLUS LEFTOVERS

⅓ cup low-sodium soy sauce	½ cup low-sodium chicken broth
3 tablespoons minced peeled fresh ginger	1 (8-ounce) can pineapple chunks in juice, drained and juice reserved
2 tablespoons packed brown sugar	
3 garlic cloves, minced	2 tablespoons red-wine vinegar
⅛ teaspoon red pepper flakes	1 tablespoon cornstarch
6 (½-pound) bone-in chicken breast halves, skinned	2 cups fresh sugar snap peas, trimmed
1 red onion, cut into ½-inch wedges through the root end	1 red bell pepper, cut into 1-inch chunks

1 Mix the soy sauce, ginger, brown sugar, garlic, and pepper flakes in a small bowl. Place the chicken and onion in a 5- or 6-quart slow cooker. Add the soy sauce mixture and turn the chicken to coat. Stir in the broth. Cover and cook until the chicken is fork-tender, 3–4 hours on high or 6–8 hours on low.

2 With a slotted spoon, transfer 2 of the chicken breast halves to a container and let cool. Cover and refrigerate up to 3 days for later use in Buffalo Chicken Salad, opposite. Transfer the remaining 4 chicken breast halves to a plate and reserve.

3 Whisk together the pineapple juice, vinegar, and cornstarch in a small bowl. Add the cornstarch mixture, peas, and bell pepper to the slow cooker, stirring to combine. Cover and cook on high until the vegetables are crisp-tender and the sauce thickens slightly, 15 minutes. Stir in the pineapple and the reserved 4 chicken breast halves. Cover and cook on high until heated through, 5 minutes.

PER SERVING (1 chicken breast half with 1⅓ cups vegetable-sauce mixture): 285 Cal, 5 g Fat, 2 g Sat Fat, 0 g Trans Fat, 83 mg Chol, 560 mg Sod, 26 g Carb, 3 g Fib, 34 g Prot, 57 mg Calc. *POINTS* value: *6.*

Buffalo Chicken Salad

prep 15 MIN • cook NONE • serves 4

2	reserved cooked chicken breast halves from Tropical Chicken (opposite)
2	tablespoons + ¼ cup fat-free ranch salad dressing
2	teaspoons hot pepper sauce

8	cups mixed salad greens
2	celery stalks, sliced
1	cup shredded carrots
½	cup crumbled reduced-fat blue cheese

1 Remove the chicken from the bones and shred the meat; transfer to a medium bowl. Stir in 2 tablespoons of the dressing and the pepper sauce.

2 Toss the salad greens, celery, and carrots in a large bowl; divide among 4 plates. Top evenly with the chicken mixture, the remaining ¼ cup of dressing, and the cheese.

PER SERVING (about 2 cups salad greens with ¾ cup chicken, 1 tablespoon dressing, and 2 tablespoons cheese): 223 Cal, 6 g Fat, 4 g Sat Fat, 0 g Trans Fat, 56 mg Chol, 764 mg Sod, 17 g Carb, 3 g Fib, 21 g Prot, 183 mg Calc. *POINTS* value: *4.*

Spanish Chicken and Rice

prep 15 MIN • cook 3–4 HRS ON HIGH • serves 4 PLUS LEFTOVERS

6 (5-ounce) boneless skinless chicken thighs	**½** teaspoon dried oregano
¼ teaspoon salt	**⅛** teaspoon red pepper flakes
1 onion, chopped	**1** (8-ounce) package yellow rice mix
1 (14-ounce) can low-sodium chicken broth	**½** cup frozen peas, thawed
1 red bell pepper, cut into 1-inch chunks	**⅓** cup sliced pimiento-stuffed green olives
2 garlic cloves, minced	

1 Sprinkle the chicken with the salt. Spray a large nonstick skillet with nonstick spray and set over medium-high heat. Cook the chicken until browned, turning once, about 8 minutes. Transfer the chicken to a 5- or 6-quart slow cooker.

2 Add the onion to the skillet. Cook, stirring, until lightly browned, about 3 minutes. Stir in the broth, bell pepper, garlic, oregano, and pepper flakes. Pour over the chicken. Cover and cook until the chicken is fork tender, 3–4 hours on high or 6–8 hours on low.

3 With a slotted spoon, transfer 2 of the chicken thighs to a container and let cool. Cover and refrigerate up to 3 days for later use in Salsa Chicken Wraps, opposite. Transfer the remaining 4 chicken thighs to a plate and reserve.

4 Stir the rice mix into the liquid in the slow cooker. Cover and cook on high until the liquid is absorbed and the rice is tender, 45 minutes. Transfer 1 cup of the rice to a microwavable bowl and let cool. Cover and refrigerate up to 3 days for use in Salsa Chicken Wraps, opposite. Add the reserved chicken thighs and the peas to the slow cooker. Cover and cook until heated through, about 10 minutes. Sprinkle with the olives.

PER SERVING (1 thigh and 1 cup rice): 443 Cal, 13 g Fat, 4 g Sat Fat, 0 g Trans Fat, 88 mg Chol, 1175 mg Sod, 43 g Carb, 3 g Fib, 37 g Prot, 94 mg Calc. **POINTS** value: **9.**

Salsa Chicken Wraps

prep 10 MIN • microwave 2 MIN • serves 4

2 reserved cooked chicken thighs and 1 cup cooked rice from Spanish Chicken and Rice (opposite)

4 (8-inch) multigrain tortillas

2 cups shredded romaine lettuce

1 small avocado, pitted, peeled, and sliced

½ cup salsa

½ cup shredded fat-free pepper-jack cheese

1 Remove the chicken from the bones and shred; discard the bones. Cover the rice with plastic wrap; then prick a few holes in the plastic. Microwave on High until hot, 1 minute. Warm the tortillas according to the package directions.

2 Place the tortillas on a work surface and spoon one-fourth of the chicken down the center of each; top each with ½ cup of the lettuce, ¼ cup of the rice, ¼ of the avocado slices, 2 tablespoons of the salsa, and 2 tablespoons of the cheese. Fold the short sides over the filling, then roll up jelly-roll-style to enclose the filling.

PER SERVING (1 wrap): 366 Cal, 13 g Fat, 3 g Sat Fat, 0 g Trans Fat, 47 mg Chol, 800 mg Sod, 38 g Carb, 6 g Fib, 25 g Prot, 210 mg Calc. **POINTS** value: **8.**

Spicy Chicken Stew

prep 15 MIN • cook 4–5 HRS ON HIGH • serves 4 PLUS LEFTOVERS

12 skinless chicken drumsticks (about 3½ pounds)	½ teaspoon ground cumin
½ teaspoon salt	¼ teaspoon cayenne
4 carrots, cut into 1-inch chunks	1 (8-ounce) can tomato sauce
1 onion, chopped	1 zucchini, halved lengthwise and sliced
3 garlic cloves, minced	¼ cup plain fat-free Greek yogurt
1 teaspoon curry powder	1 tablespoon peanut butter

1 Sprinkle the chicken with the salt. Spray a large nonstick skillet with nonstick spray and heat over medium-high heat. Add the chicken and cook, turning occasionally, until browned, about 10 minutes. Transfer the chicken to a 5- or 6-quart slow cooker. Add the carrots to the slow cooker.

2 Add the onion to the skillet and reduce the heat to medium. Cook, stirring occasionally, until softened, about 4 minutes. Add the garlic, curry powder, cumin, and cayenne and cook, stirring for 1 minute. Stir in the tomato sauce. Pour over the chicken. Cover and cook until the chicken is tender, 4–5 hours on high or 8–10 hours on low.

3 With a slotted spoon, transfer 4 of the drumsticks to a container and let cool. Cover and refrigerate up to 3 days for use in Chicken Fried Rice, opposite. Transfer the remaining 8 drumsticks to a plate and reserve.

4 Spray a large nonstick skillet with nonstick spray and place over medium-high heat. Add the zucchini and cook, stirring frequently, until lightly browned, about 5 minutes. Add the zucchini to the slow cooker. Cover and cook on high until tender, about 10 minutes. Whisk the yogurt and peanut butter in a small bowl until smooth; add to the slow cooker, stirring to combine. Return the reserved drumsticks to the slow cooker; cover and cook on high until hot, about 10 minutes.

PER SERVING (2 drumsticks with generous ¾ cup vegetables and sauce): 239 Cal, 6 g Fat, 2 g Sat Fat, 0 g Trans Fat, 99 mg Chol, 641 mg Sod, 16 g Carb, 4 g Fib, 30 g Prot, 105 mg Calc. **POINTS** value: **4.**

...then this! # Chicken Fried Rice

prep 5 MIN • cook 15 MIN • serves 4

1¾ cups water

1 cup instant brown rice

2 cups small broccoli florets

4 reserved cooked chicken drumsticks from Spicy Chicken Stew (opposite)

2 large eggs, lightly beaten

1 teaspoon canola oil

¾ cup shredded carrots

3 scallions, sliced

2 teaspoons minced peeled fresh ginger

2 tablespoons reduced-sodium soy sauce

¼ teaspoon salt

1 Bring the water and rice to a boil in a Dutch oven. Reduce the heat; cover and simmer 6 minutes. Stir in the broccoli; cover and simmer until the water is absorbed, about 4 minutes.

2 Meanwhile, remove the chicken from the bones and cut into bite-size pieces.

3 Spray a large nonstick skillet with nonstick spray and heat over medium heat. Add the eggs and cook, stirring constantly, until scrambled, about 1 minute. Transfer to a plate. Wipe out the skillet.

4 Add the oil to the skillet and place over medium-high heat. Add the chicken, carrots, scallions, and ginger. Cook, stirring constantly, until the chicken is heated through, 2 minutes. Add the rice mixture, the eggs, soy sauce, and salt; cook, stirring constantly, 1 minute.

PER SERVING (scant 1½ cups): 241 Cal, 7 g Fat, 2 g Sat Fat, 0 g Trans Fat, 155 mg Chol, 612 mg Sod, 25 g Carb, 5 g Fib, 20 g Prot, 69 mg Calc. **POINTS** value: **5.**

In the Kitchen

Instant brown rice is a handy ingredient to keep in the pantry. It cooks in about 10 minutes and is an easy way to add whole grains to weeknight dinners.

Tuscan Braised Turkey

prep 10 MIN • cook 3–4 HRS ON HIGH • serves 4 PLUS LEFTOVERS

1   tablespoon chopped fresh rosemary

2   teaspoons chopped fresh thyme

½   teaspoon salt

1   (3-pound) bone-in skin-on turkey breast half

1   (15½-ounce) can cannellini beans, rinsed and drained

1   pint grape tomatoes

1   small onion, finely chopped

1   garlic clove, minced

½   cup low-sodium chicken broth

1 Mix the rosemary, thyme, and salt in a bowl; reserve ½ teaspoon of the herb mixture. With fingers, loosen the skin on the turkey breast, leaving the skin attached. Rub the remaining herb mixture on the meat under the skin.

2 Place the turkey, skin side down, in a 5- or 6-quart slow cooker. Mix the beans, tomatoes, onion, garlic, and the reserved ½ teaspoon herb mixture in a bowl. Pour over the turkey and add the broth. Cover and cook until an instant-read thermometer inserted into the center of the turkey registers 165°F, 3–4 hours on high or 6–8 hours on low. Remove the turkey to a plate; cover with foil and let stand 15 minutes.

3 Pour the bean mixture into a large saucepan and bring to a boil. Reduce the heat slightly and boil, stirring occasionally, until reduced to 2½ cups, about 10 minutes. Remove and discard the turkey skin. Remove the breast from the bone and cut in half. Transfer one half to a container and let cool. Cover and refrigerate up to 3 days for use in Turkey Tonnato, opposite. Cut the remaining turkey into 8 slices and serve with the bean mixture.

PER SERVING (2 slices turkey with generous ½ cup bean mixture): 275 Cal, 2 g Fat, 1 g Sat Fat, 0 g Trans Fat, 89 mg Chol, 510 mg Sod, 24 g Carb, 6 g Fib, 40 g Prot, 101 mg Calc. *POINTS* value: *5.*

Turkey Tonnato

prep 15 MIN • cook NONE • serves 4

¼ cup fat-free mayonnaise

¼ cup plain fat-free Greek yogurt

1 (3-ounce) can light tuna in water, drained

2 tablespoons water

1 tablespoon fresh lemon juice

3 teaspoons capers, drained

¼ teaspoon salt

Reserved cooked turkey from Tuscan Braised Turkey (opposite)

8 cups salad greens

2 tomatoes, cut into wedges

½ cucumber, peeled and sliced

1 To make the sauce, combine the mayonnaise, yogurt, tuna, water, lemon juice, 2 teaspoons of the capers, and the salt in a food processor. Process until smooth.

2 Cut the turkey into 8 slices. Arrange the salad greens on 4 plates. Top each serving with 2 slices of the turkey and ¼ cup of the sauce. Arrange the tomatoes and cucumber evenly on the side; sprinkle evenly with the remaining 1 teaspoon capers. Serve at once.

PER SERVING (1 plate): 224 Cal, 2 g Fat, 1 g Sat Fat, 0 g Trans Fat, 97 mg Chol, 657 mg Sod, 10 g Carb, 4 g Fib, 40 g Prot, 115 mg Calc. **POINTS** value: **4.**

make this... # BBQ Turkey

prep 15 MIN • cook 5–6 HRS ON HIGH • serves 4 PLUS LEFTOVERS

1 **onion, chopped**	1 **tablespoon Worcestershire sauce**
½ **cup ketchup**	
½ **cup chili sauce**	4 **(1-pound) turkey thighs, skinned**
¼ **cup apple-cider vinegar**	
2 **tablespoons packed brown sugar**	2 **large sweet potatoes, peeled and cut into 2-inch chunks**
2 **tablespoons spicy brown mustard**	1 **(10-ounce) box frozen lima beans**

1 Mix the onion, ketchup, chili sauce, vinegar, brown sugar, mustard, and Worcestershire sauce in a 5- or 6-quart slow cooker. Add the turkey; place the potatoes and lima beans around the turkey. Cover and cook until the turkey is fork-tender, 5–6 hours on high or 10–12 hours on low.

2 With a slotted spoon, transfer 2 of the turkey thighs to a container. Transfer ½ cup of the potatoes and ½ cup of the lima beans to separate containers and let cool. Cover and refrigerate up to 3 days for later use in Turkey and Shrimp Gumbo, opposite.

3 Transfer the remaining 2 turkey thighs to a plate and reserve. Transfer the remaining 3 cups of vegetables to a bowl; cover and keep warm.

4 Transfer the sauce remaining in the slow cooker to a medium saucepan and bring to a boil over medium-high heat. Cook, stirring frequently, until reduced to 2 cups, 10 minutes.

5 Remove the meat from the bones of the reserved turkey. Cut the turkey into small slices and serve with the reserved vegetables and sauce.

PER SERVING (about ½ cup turkey with ½ cup sauce and generous ¾ cup vegetables): 412 Cal, 6 g Fat, 2 g Sat Fat, 0 g Trans Fat, 140 mg Chol, 1,075 mg Sod, 45 g Carb, 7 g Fib, 42 g Prot, 98 mg Calc. **POINTS** value: **8.**

Turkey and Shrimp Gumbo

prep 5 MIN • cook 15 MIN • serves 6

2 cups low-sodium chicken broth

¾ cup instant brown rice

2 reserved cooked turkey thighs, ½ cup cooked sweet potatoes, and ½ cup lima beans from BBQ Turkey (opposite)

1 (14½-ounce) can diced tomatoes with green pepper, celery, and onions

1 teaspoon Cajun seasoning

¼ teaspoon dried thyme

½ pound medium shrimp, peeled and deveined

3 scallions, sliced

1 Mix the broth and rice in a Dutch oven; cover and bring to a boil. Meanwhile, remove the meat from the bones of the reserved turkey. Cut the turkey into bite-size pieces. Dice the potatoes.

2 Add the turkey, potatoes, lima beans, tomatoes, Cajun seasoning, and thyme to the rice mixture; cover and return to a boil. Reduce the heat; cover and simmer, stirring occasionally, until the rice is tender, 8 minutes.

3 Stir in the shrimp and return to a boil. Reduce the heat; cover and simmer just until the shrimp are opaque in the center, 1–2 minutes. Stir in the scallions.

PER SERVING (scant 1 cup): 267 Cal, 5 g Fat, 2 g Sat Fat, 0 g Trans Fat, 147 mg Chol, 360 mg Sod, 20 g Carb, 4 g Fib, 34 g Prot, 77 mg Calc. **POINTS** value: **5.**

chapter 5
Go Vegetarian

Lemony Tofu Caesar Salad 144
Thai Tofu and Vegetable Stir-Fry 145

Veggie Tofu Burgers 146
Stuffed Bell Peppers with Tomato-Basil Sauce 147

Edamame-Zucchini Sauté 148
Balsamic Vegetable and Tofu Salad 149

Sesame Edamame Salad 150
Double Soy Soup 151

Easy Chickpea Curry 152
Chickpea-Vegetable Salad 153

Cannellini Beans and Swiss Chard with Ricotta 154
Quinoa with Swiss Chard and Almonds 155

Sweet Potato and Chickpea Salad 156
Sweet Potato Falafel Sandwiches 157

Spiced Three-Bean Stew 158
Cajun Bean Nachos 159

Lemon-Honey Beans and Carrots 160
Raspberry Wild Rice and Bean Salad 161

Middle Eastern-Style Lentils and Rice 162
Lentil Soup with Yogurt-Cilantro Topping 163

Polenta with Tomato Sauce 164
Savory Baked Eggs 165

Cheese Ravioli with Roasted Cauliflower 166
Cauliflower Frittata 167

Hungarian Pepper Stew with Noodles 168
Bell Pepper Tabbouleh Salad 169

Gnocchi with Tomato and Parmesan 170
Grape Tomato Clafouti 171

Roasted Corn Chowder 172
Skillet Corn and Bean Chilaquiles 173

Butternut Squash Soup 174
Vegetable-Barley Risotto 175

Roasted Beet and Goat Cheese Salad with Mint 176
Roasted Beet and White Bean Soup 177

make this... Lemony Tofu Caesar Salad

prep 15 MIN • cook 6 MIN • serves 4 PLUS LEFTOVERS

3 garlic cloves, peeled	**6** slices whole-wheat baguette (1½ ounces)
Grated zest and juice of 1 large lemon	**12** cups torn romaine lettuce
¼ cup + ⅓ cup light Caesar dressing	**1½** cups cherry tomatoes, halved
2 (12-ounce) containers reduced-fat firm tofu, sliced lengthwise in half	**¼** cup shaved Parmesan cheese

1 Chop 2 cloves of the garlic and place in a zip-close plastic bag with the lemon zest, 2 tablespoons of the lemon juice, and ¼ cup of the dressing; add the tofu. Squeeze out the air and seal the bag; turn to coat the tofu. Refrigerate, turning the bag once, 30 minutes.

2 Spray the grill rack with nonstick spray and prepare a medium hot fire. Remove the tofu from the marinade; lightly coat the tofu with nonstick spray. Lightly coat the bread with nonstick spray.

3 Place the tofu and the bread on the grill rack. Grill the tofu until golden, 3–4 minutes on each side. Grill the bread until lightly toasted, 1–2 minutes on each side. Cut the remaining garlic clove in half and rub both sides of each bread slice with a cut side of the garlic. Transfer half of the tofu (2 pieces) to a container and let cool. Cover and refrigerate up to 3 days for later use in Thai Tofu and Vegetable Stir-Fry, opposite. Cut the remaining tofu and bread into ½-inch cubes.

4 Toss together the lettuce, tomatoes, and the remaining ⅓ cup of dressing in a large bowl. Place the salad on a platter; top with the tofu, bread cubes, and cheese. Serve at once.

PER SERVING (3½ cups): 253 Cal, 14 g Fat, 3 g Sat Fat, 0 g Trans Fat, 37 mg Chol, 423 mg Sod, 21 g Carb, 7 g Fib, 14 g Prot, 204 mg Calc. **POINTS** value: **5.**

Thai Tofu and Vegetable Stir-Fry

prep 10 MIN · cook 12 MIN · serves 4

2	teaspoons canola oil
1	small sweet onion, thinly sliced
2	(16-ounce) packages frozen stir-fry vegetables
2	teaspoons grated peeled fresh ginger
2	reserved cooked tofu pieces from Lemony Tofu Caesar Salad (opposite), cut into ½-inch cubes

2	tablespoons bottled stir-fry sauce
1½	teaspoons Asian fish sauce
1	teaspoon honey
½	cup chopped fresh cilantro
1	lime, cut into 4 wedges

1 Heat a nonstick wok or large deep nonstick skillet over medium-high heat until a drop of water sizzles on it. Pour in the oil and swirl to coat the wok; then add the onion. Stir-fry until softened, 4 minutes.

2 Add the stir-fry vegetables and ginger; stir-fry until the vegetables are thawed, 6 minutes. Add the tofu, stir-fry sauce, fish sauce, and honey and cook, stirring constantly, until the mixture comes to a boil and the tofu is heated through, 1 minute. Remove from the heat and stir in the cilantro. Serve with the lime wedges.

PER SERVING (1½ cups): 232 Cal, 9 g Fat, 1 g Sat Fat, 0 g Trans Fat, 9 mg Chol, 349 mg Sod, 30 g Carb, 9 g Fib, 14 g Prot, 124 mg Calc. *POINTS* value: **5.**

make this... Veggie Tofu Burgers

prep 20 MIN • cook 30 MIN • serves 4 PLUS LEFTOVERS

1	(12-ounce) package reduced-fat firm tofu
2	carrots, cut into 1-inch chunks
1	large onion, cut into 1-inch chunks
1	cup quartered fresh mushrooms
½	cup water
¼	cup bulgur
1	tablespoon dried Italian seasoning

½	cup barbecue sauce
2	tablespoons mild cayenne pepper sauce
¾	teaspoon salt
1	(15-ounce) can chickpeas, rinsed and drained
½	cup plain dried bread crumbs
2	large eggs

1 Place the tofu on a large plate. Set another plate on top and weight down with a heavy pan. Let stand 15 minutes. Drain and discard the liquid.

2 Meanwhile, put the carrots in a food processor and pulse until coarsely chopped. Add the onion and mushrooms and pulse until the mixture is finely chopped. Do not clean the food processor.

3 Place the chopped vegetables, water, bulgur, and Italian seasoning in a large nonstick skillet; bring to a boil. Reduce the heat; cover and cook, stirring occasionally, until the vegetables are tender, 15 minutes. Stir in the barbecue sauce, pepper sauce, and salt. Cook, uncovered, stirring occasionally, until the mixture is dry, 5 minutes. Transfer the mixture to a large bowl and let stand 10 minutes to cool slightly.

4 Put the chickpeas in the food processor and pulse until finely chopped. Break the tofu into pieces and add to the food processor. Add the bread crumbs and pulse until the mixture is crumbly. Add the chickpea mixture to the vegetable mixture; stir in the eggs. Transfer 3 cups of the mixture to a container; cover and refrigerate up to 3 days for later use in Stuffed Bell Peppers with Tomato-Basil Sauce, opposite. Form the remaining mixture into 4 patties.

5 Spray a large nonstick skillet with olive oil nonstick spray and set over medium heat. Add the patties and cook until browned, 3–4 minutes on each side.

PER SERVING (1 burger): 199 Cal, 5 g Fat, 1 g Sat Fat, 0 g Trans Fat, 53 mg Chol, 609 mg Sod, 31 g Carb, 6 g Fib, 10 g Prot, 85 mg Calc. *POINTS* value: *4.*

Stuffed Bell Peppers with Tomato-Basil Sauce

prep 10 MIN • microwave 10 MIN • serves 4

4 green, red, or yellow bell peppers, tops cut off and seeded	**1** cup frozen corn kernels
	1 cup frozen peas
3 cups reserved cooked chickpea mixture from Veggie Tofu Burgers (opposite)	**¾** cup light tomato-basil pasta sauce

1 Trim the bottom of the peppers so they set level. Place the bell peppers, bottom side up, in a large microwavable dish. Cover with plastic wrap; then prick a few holes in the plastic. Microwave on High 3 minutes.

2 Meanwhile, stir together the chickpea mixture, corn, peas, and ¼ cup of the pasta sauce in a large bowl. With tongs, turn the peppers top side up. Spoon the chickpea mixture into the peppers.

3 Spoon the remaining ½ cup of sauce over the peppers. Cover with plastic wrap; then prick a few holes in the plastic. Microwave on High until the filling is heated through, 5 minutes. Let stand 10 minutes before serving.

PER SERVING (1 stuffed pepper): 355 Cal, 8 g Fat, 1 g Sat Fat, 0 g Trans Fat, 53 mg Chol, 822 mg Sod, 58k g Carb, 11 g Fib, 18 g Prot, 137 mg Calc. **POINTS** value: **7.**

In the Kitchen

When you trim the bottoms of the peppers, make sure you don't cut completely through the pepper or the filling will fall out of the bottom.

make this... Edamame-Zucchini Sauté

prep 15 MIN • cook 15 MIN • serves 4 PLUS LEFTOVERS

3 tablespoons reduced-sodium soy sauce	1 pound broccoli, cut into small florets
2 tablespoons rice vinegar	4 zucchini, halved lengthwise and sliced
2 teaspoons honey	2 cups frozen shelled edamame (green soybeans)
2 teaspoons hoisin or barbecue sauce	1 (12-ounce) package 5-spice marinated firm tofu,
1½ teaspoons cornstarch	drained and cut into ½-inch cubes
2 teaspoons sesame oil	1 tablespoon sesame seeds
1 large onion, coarsely chopped	

1 Stir together the soy sauce, vinegar, honey, hoisin sauce, and cornstarch in a small bowl until blended and reserve.

2 Heat the oil in a nonstick Dutch oven over medium-high heat. Add the onion and broccoli; cook, stirring occasionally, 6 minutes. Add the zucchini and cook, stirring occasionally, 4 minutes. Add the edamame and cook, stirring occasionally, until the vegetables are crisp-tender, 2 minutes.

3 Remove the Dutch oven from the heat. Transfer 4 cups of the vegetables to a container and let cool.

4 Return the Dutch oven to medium-high heat. Add the soy sauce mixture and 2 cups of the tofu. Cook, stirring constantly, until the mixture boils and thickens, 1–2 minutes. Sprinkle with the sesame seeds.

5 Add the remaining ¾ cup of tofu to the reserved vegetable mixture; cover and refrigerate up to 3 days for later use in Balsamic Vegetable and Tofu Salad, opposite.

PER SERVING (1¾ cups): 230 Cal, 9 g Fat, 2 g Sat Fat, 0 g Trans Fat, 0 mg Chol, 644 mg Sod, 24 g Carb, 7 g Fib, 16 g Prot, 121 mg Calc. *POINTS* value: *5.*

Balsamic Vegetable and Tofu Salad

prep 15 MIN • cook NONE • serves 4

4 cups reserved cooked vegetables and ¾ cup reserved tofu from Edamame-Zucchini Sauté (opposite)

3 carrots, shredded

2 cups grape or cherry tomatoes, halved

1 yellow or red bell pepper, cut into 1-inch strips

⅓ cup reduced-fat balsamic dressing

⅛ teaspoon salt

⅛ teaspoon black pepper

Drain and discard any liquid from the vegetables and tofu; place in a large bowl. Add the remaining ingredients and toss to combine.

PER SERVING (1¾ cups): 174 Cal, 7 g Fat, 1 g Sat Fat, 0 g Trans Fat, 0 mg Chol, 399 mg Sod, 22 g Carb, 6 g Fib, 9 g Prot, 88 mg Calc. **POINTS** value: **1.**

◆ Filling Extra

Add 2½ cups cooked whole-wheat penne when you toss the salad together. The per-serving **POINTS** value will increase by **1.**

make this... Sesame Edamame Salad

prep 15 MIN • cook 5 MIN • serves 2 PLUS LEFTOVERS

1 (14-ounce) package frozen shelled edamame (green soybeans)

1 cup frozen peas, thawed

1 celery stalk with leaves, finely chopped

3 scallions, thinly sliced

¼ cup seasoned rice vinegar

2 teaspoons Asian (dark) sesame oil

¼ teaspoon salt

⅛ teaspoon black pepper

2 small bunches watercress, trimmed

1 Cook the edamame according to the package directions; drain. Rinse under cold running water until cool and drain well.

2 Transfer the edamame to a large bowl. Add the peas, celery, scallions, vinegar, oil, salt, and pepper; mix well. Transfer 1 cup of the edamame mixture to a container. Cover and refrigerate up to 2 days for later use in Double Soy Soup, opposite.

3 Place the watercress on a platter; top with the remaining 3 cups of edamame mixture.

PER SERVING (generous 1½ cups edamame mixture with 2 cups watercress): 296 Cal, 12 g Fat, 2 g Sat Fat, 0 g Trans Fat, 0 mg Chol, 670 mg Sod, 32 g Carb, 10 g Fib, 20 g Prot, 218 mg Calc. **POINTS** value: **6.**

Double Soy Soup

prep 10 MIN • cook 10 MIN • serves 4

4   cups low-sodium vegetable broth
2   scallions, thinly sliced
2   mushrooms, thinly sliced
¼   teaspoon salt
⅛   teaspoon black pepper
1½   cups diced firm tofu
1   cup reserved edamame mixture from Sesame Edamame Salad (opposite)
¼   cup fresh cilantro leaves

1 Mix the broth, scallions, mushrooms, salt, and pepper in a large saucepan. Bring just to a boil over medium heat.

2 Add the tofu, edamame mixture, and cilantro; return to a boil. Reduce the heat and simmer, stirring gently, until heated through, 2 minutes.

PER SERVING (1¾ cups): 131 Cal, 6 g Fat, 1 g Sat Fat, 0 g Trans Fat, 0 mg Chol, 530 mg Sod, 11 g Carb, 3 g Fib, 12 g Prot, 224 mg Calc. **POINTS** value: **3.**

make this... Easy Chickpea Curry

prep 15 MIN • cook 15 MIN • serves 4 PLUS LEFTOVERS

1	tablespoon olive oil	½	teaspoon salt
2	red onions, finely chopped	2	(16-ounce) cans chickpeas, rinsed and drained
2	jalapeño peppers, seeded and thinly sliced	1	(14½-ounce) can diced tomatoes
1	large garlic clove, minced	1	cup fresh cilantro leaves
2	teaspoons minced peeled fresh ginger	1	cup quinoa, rinsed
1	teaspoon ground coriander	2	cups water
½	teaspoon ground cumin		

1 Heat the oil in a large nonstick skillet over medium heat. Add the onions and cook, stirring occasionally, until crisp-tender, 2 minutes. Add the jalapeños, garlic, and ginger; cook, stirring occasionally, until fragrant, 2 minutes. Add the coriander, cumin, and salt; cook, stirring frequently, until fragrant, 30 seconds. Add the chickpeas and tomatoes; cook, stirring occasionally, until slightly thickened, 10 minutes. Stir in the cilantro.

2 Meanwhile, mix the quinoa and water in a small saucepan; bring to a boil. Reduce the heat; cover and simmer until the liquid is absorbed and the quinoa is tender, about 10 minutes. Transfer 1 cup of the chickpea mixture to a container and let cool. Cover and refrigerate up to 4 days for later use in Chickpea-Vegetable Salad, opposite.

3 Transfer the quinoa to a large bowl. Top with the remaining 4 cups of chickpea mixture.

PER SERVING (1 cup chickpea mixture with about ¾ cup quinoa): 424 Cal, 9 g Fat, 1 g Sat Fat, 0 g Trans Fat, 0 mg Chol, 545 mg Sod, 72 g Carb, 12 g Fib, 18 g Prot, 135 mg Calc. *POINTS* value: *8.*

Chickpea-Vegetable Salad

prep 15 MIN · cook 10 MIN · serves 2

3   **cups small broccoli florets**

2   **cups baby carrots**

1   **cup reserved cooked chickpea mixture from Easy Chickpea Curry (opposite)**

¾   **cup halved cherry tomatoes**

2   **teaspoons olive oil**

Juice of ¼ lemon

¼   **teaspoon salt**

⅛   **teaspoon black pepper**

1 Bring a large saucepan of lightly salted water to a boil. Add the broccoli and carrots; cook until crisp-tender, 4–5 minutes. Drain in a colander. Rinse under cold running water until cool and drain well. Transfer the vegetables to a large bowl.

2 Add the chickpea mixture, tomatoes, oil, lemon juice, salt, and pepper; mix well.

PER SERVING (about 3 cups): 280 Cal, 8 g Fat, 2 g Sat Fat, 0 g Trans Fat, 0 mg Chol, 1,032 mg Sod, 46 g Carb, 14 g Fib, 10 g Prot, 152 mg Calc. **POINTS** value: **5.**

Cannellini Beans and Swiss Chard with Ricotta

prep 15 MIN • **cook** 30 MIN • **serves** 4 PLUS LEFTOVERS

6 **vegetarian bacon strips**	4 **garlic cloves, thinly sliced**
2 **bunches Swiss chard (about 1½ pounds)**	¼ **teaspoon red pepper flakes**
3 **tablespoons thinly sliced oil-packed sun-dried tomatoes**	2 **(15-ounce) cans cannellini (white kidney) beans, rinsed and drained**
1 **teaspoon oil from sun-dried tomatoes**	2 **tablespoons balsamic vinegar**
2 **large onions, thinly sliced**	¾ **teaspoon salt**
2 **large yellow bell peppers, coarsely chopped**	¾ **cup part-skim ricotta cheese**

1 Cook the bacon according to the package directions; cool, chop, and reserve.

2 Cut away the chard leaves from the stems; cut the leaves into ½-inch strips and cut the stems into 1-inch pieces, keeping the leaves and stems separate.

3 Blot the oil from the tomatoes using paper towels and reserve.

4 Heat the oil in a large nonstick skillet over medium heat. Add the onions and cook, stirring often, until softened, 4 minutes. Stir in the Swiss chard stems, the bell peppers, garlic, and pepper flakes. Cook, stirring occasionally, until the vegetables are almost tender, 6 minutes.

5 Add the chard leaves; cook, stirring often, until tender, 6 minutes. Stir in the beans, vinegar, salt, tomatoes, and bacon. Cook until heated through, 2 minutes.

6 Transfer 3 cups of the vegetable mixture to a container and let cool. Cover and refrigerate up to 4 days for later use in Quinoa with Swiss Chard and Almonds, opposite. Spoon the remaining chard mixture into 4 bowls. Top each with 3 tablespoons of the ricotta and serve at once.

PER SERVING (1¼ cups chard mixture with 3 tablespoons ricotta): 305 Cal, 10 g Fat, 3 g Sat Fat, 0 g Trans Fat, 14 mg Chol, 827 mg Sod, 41 g Carb, 10 g Fib, 17 g Prot, 244 mg Calc. **POINTS** value: **6.**

Quinoa with Swiss Chard and Almonds

prep 10 MIN • cook 20 MIN • serves 4

1 cup quinoa, rinsed

2 cups water

1 large shallot, chopped

2 teaspoons honey

1 teaspoon ground cumin

1 teaspoon smoked paprika

¾ teaspoon salt

¼ cup sliced almonds

3 cups reserved cooked vegetable mixture from Cannellini Beans and Swiss Chard with Ricotta (opposite)

¼ cup golden raisins

1 tablespoon red-wine vinegar

1 Place the quinoa in a medium saucepan over medium-high heat. Toast, stirring constantly, until dry, lightly browned, and fragrant, about 4 minutes. Carefully add the water; stir in the shallot, honey, cumin, paprika, and salt. Bring to a boil; reduce the heat, cover, and simmer until the quinoa is tender, 12 minutes.

2 Meanwhile, place the almonds in a small skillet over medium heat. Toast, stirring constantly, until golden and fragrant, 3 minutes. Transfer to a plate to cool.

3 Stir the chard mixture, raisins, and vinegar into the quinoa; cook until heated through, 3 minutes. Top with the almonds.

PER SERVING (1¼ cups quinoa mixture with 1 tablespoon almonds): 388 Cal, 9 g Fat, 1 g Sat Fat, 0 g Trans Fat, 0 mg Chol, 871 mg Sod, 67 g Carb, 9 g Fib, 15 g Prot, 133 mg Calc. **POINTS** value: **8.**

In the Kitchen

Quinoa is a delicately-flavored whole grain that cooks up in about 10 minutes. Always rinse quinoa before cooking to remove a naturally-occurring bitter-tasting residue on the grain.

make this... Sweet Potato and Chickpea Salad

prep 20 MIN • bake 25 MIN • serves 4 PLUS LEFTOVERS

2 pounds sweet potatoes, peeled and diced	**¼** teaspoon black pepper
2 tablespoons seasoned rice vinegar	**1** (15-ounce) can chickpeas, rinsed and drained
1 tablespoon olive oil	**½** cup fresh cilantro leaves
1 tablespoon minced peeled fresh ginger	**4** cups baby arugula
1 garlic clove, minced	**¼** cup crumbled low-fat goat cheese
½ teaspoon salt	

1 Preheat the oven to 450°F. Spray a large rimmed baking sheet with nonstick spray. Spread the potatoes on the prepared baking sheet. Bake until fork-tender, 25 minutes, stirring twice during cooking.

2 Meanwhile, to make the dressing, combine the vinegar, oil, ginger, garlic, salt, and pepper in a large bowl; whisk until blended.

3 Add the potatoes, chickpeas, and cilantro to the dressing; toss to coat. Transfer 2 cups of the potato mixture to a container and let cool. Cover and refrigerate up to 3 days for later use in Sweet Potato Falafel Sandwiches, opposite. Place the arugula on a platter; top with the remaining 4 cups of potato mixture and sprinkle with the cheese.

PER SERVING (1 cup potato mixture, 1 cup arugula, and 1 tablespoon cheese): 218 Cal, 5 g Fat, 2 g Sat Fat, 0 g Trans Fat, 3 mg Chol, 447 mg Sod, 36 g Carb, 6 g Fib, 8 g Prot, 93 mg Calc. *POINTS* value: *4.*

Sweet Potato Falafel Sandwiches

prep 15 MIN • bake 25 MIN • serves 4

2 cups reserved cooked potato mixture from Sweet Potato and Chickpea Salad (opposite)

1½ tablespoons sesame seeds

1½ tablespoons plain dried bread crumbs

½ cup plain fat-free yogurt

½ teaspoon chili powder

4 (6-inch) whole-wheat pitas

2 cups baby salad greens

12 cherry tomatoes, halved

1 Preheat the oven to 400°F. Spray a baking sheet with nonstick spray.

2 Puree the potato mixture in a food processor or blender. Form into 4 (½-inch-thick) patties.

3 Mix the sesame seeds and bread crumbs on a plate. Coat each patty with the crumb mixture and transfer to the prepared baking sheet. Bake until heated through, 25 minutes.

4 Meanwhile, to make the sauce, mix the yogurt and chili powder in a small bowl.

5 Fill each of the pitas with 1 falafel, ½ cup of the greens, and 3 of the halved cherry tomatoes. Serve with the sauce.

PER SERVING (1 falafel sandwich with 2 tablespoons sauce): 305 Cal, 6 g Fat, 1 g Sat Fat, 0 g Trans Fat, 1 mg Chol, 537 mg Sod, 55 g Carb, 9 g Fib, 12 g Prot, 126 mg Calc.
POINTS value: **6.**

Spiced Three-Bean Stew

prep 15 MIN • cook 45 MIN • serves 4 PLUS LEFTOVERS

1	tablespoon olive oil		½	teaspoon salt
2	large onions, chopped		**2**	cups frozen French green beans
4	garlic cloves, minced		¼	cup raisins
1	(1-pound) bag frozen sliced bell peppers		½	teaspoon ground cumin
2	(14½-ounce) cans fire-roasted diced tomatoes		½	teaspoon cinnamon
2	(15-ounce) cans black beans, rinsed and drained		⅛	teaspoon cayenne
1	(15-ounce) can red kidney beans, rinsed and drained			

1 Heat the oil in a Dutch oven over medium heat. Add the onions and garlic; cook, stirring frequently, until tender, 10 minutes. Add the bell peppers and tomatoes; bring to a boil. Reduce the heat and simmer until slightly thickened, 15 minutes. Stir in the black beans, kidney beans, and salt. Cook, stirring occasionally, until heated through, 5 minutes.

2 Transfer 4½ cups of the bean mixture to a container and let cool. Cover and refrigerate up to 4 days for later use in Cajun Bean Nachos, opposite.

3 Add the green beans, raisins, cumin, cinnamon, and cayenne to the remaining bean mixture; bring to a boil. Reduce the heat; cover and simmer, stirring occasionally, until the green beans are tender and the flavors are blended, 10 minutes.

PER SERVING (1½ cups): 257 Cal, 3 g Fat, 0 g Sat Fat, 0 g Trans Fat, 0 mg Chol, 663 mg Sod, 50 g Carb, 15 g Fib, 12 g Prot, 145 mg Calc. **POINTS** value: **5.**

Cajun Bean Nachos

prep 10 MIN • cook/broil 10 MIN • serves 4

4½ cups reserved cooked bean mixture from Spiced Three-Bean Stew (opposite)

1 tablespoon salt-free extra-spicy seasoning blend

32 baked tortilla chips (about 3 ounces)

½ cup shredded fat-free cheddar cheese

2 tablespoons canned chopped green chiles

2 plum tomatoes, diced

2 scallions, thinly sliced

1 Preheat the broiler. Line a rimmed baking sheet with foil.

2 Mix the bean stew and seasoning blend in a medium saucepan and set over medium heat. Cook, stirring occasionally, until heated through, 8 minutes.

3 Spread the tortilla chips on the prepared baking sheet. Spoon the bean mixture evenly over the chips. Sprinkle with the cheese and chiles. Broil 4 inches from the heat until the cheese is melted, 2 minutes. Top with the tomatoes and scallions.

PER SERVING (8 tortilla chips with about 1¼ cups topping): 328 Cal, 3 g Fat, 1 g Sat Fat, 0 g Trans Fat, 2 mg Chol, 997 mg Sod, 60 g Carb, 14 g Fib, 17 g Prot, 242 mg Calc. **POINTS** value: **6.**

Lemon-Honey Beans and Carrots

prep 30 MIN • cook 30 MIN • serves 4 PLUS LEFTOVERS

1	(16-ounce) package frozen baby lima beans	1	cup water
1	teaspoon salt	½	cup dry white wine
2	pounds green beans, trimmed and cut into 2-inch pieces	2	tablespoons honey
		2	teaspoons butter
1	pound baby carrots, quartered lengthwise	¼	teaspoon black pepper
4	large shallots, sliced	1	teaspoon cornstarch
4	(1 x 3-inch) strips lemon peel, cut into thin slices	3	tablespoons lemon juice

1 Bring a large saucepan of water to a boil. Add the lima beans and ½ teaspoon of the salt. Return to a boil and cook 8 minutes. Add the green beans and cook until the beans are crisp-tender, 6 minutes. Drain in a colander. Transfer 5 cups of the bean mixture to a bowl and reserve. Rinse the remaining 3 cups of bean mixture under cold running water until cool. Drain and transfer to a container; cover and refrigerate up to 2 days for later use in Raspberry Wild Rice and Bean Salad, opposite.

2 Meanwhile, mix the carrots, shallots, lemon peel, ½ cup of the water, the wine, and 1 tablespoon of the honey in a large nonstick skillet. Bring to a boil. Reduce the heat and simmer, covered, 10 minutes. Increase the heat to medium-high and cook, uncovered, until the carrots are tender and most of the liquid has evaporated, 5 minutes. Add the reserved 5 cups of the bean mixture, the butter, pepper, and the remaining ½ teaspoon of salt and 1 tablespoon of honey.

3 Stir together the remaining ½ cup of water and the cornstarch in a small bowl until blended. Add to the vegetable mixture; cook, stirring constantly, until the mixture thickens, 1 minute. Stir in the lemon juice.

PER SERVING (2 cups): 242 Cal, 3 g Fat, 1 g Sat Fat, 0 g Trans Fat, 5 mg Chol, 639 mg Sod, 50 g Carb, 12 g Fib, 9 g Prot, 125 mg Calc. *POINTS* value: *4.*

Raspberry Wild Rice and Bean Salad

prep 10 MIN • cook NONE • serves 4

3 cups reserved cooked bean mixture from Lemon-Honey Beans and Carrots (opposite)	**¾** cup diced celery
1 large yellow or red bell pepper, diced	**½** cup reduced-fat raspberry vinaigrette
1 cup red seedless grapes, halved	**1** tablespoon white-wine vinegar
1 (8.8-ounce) package cooked brown-and-wild rice blend (about 1¾ cups)	

Toss together all the ingredients in a large bowl.

PER SERVING (1½ cups): 228 Cal, 5 g Fat, 1 g Sat Fat, 0 g Trans Fat, 0 mg Chol, 638 mg Sod, 42 g Carb, 7 g Fib, 7 g Prot, 63 mg Calc. **POINTS** value: **4.**

In the Kitchen

When you cut the lemon peel to make the Lemon-Honey Beans and Carrots, cut the strips as thin as possible to get only the yellow peel and not the white bitter-tasting pith.

Middle Eastern-Style Lentils and Rice

prep 15 MIN • cook 45 MIN • serves 4 PLUS LEFTOVERS

6 **cups water**	⅛ **teaspoon cayenne**
2 **cups lentils, picked over and rinsed**	1 **cup shredded carrots**
1 **cup long-grain white rice**	1 **cup fresh cilantro leaves**
1 **teaspoon ground cumin**	1 **tablespoon olive oil**
½ **teaspoon ground allspice**	3 **red onions, thinly sliced**
¾ **teaspoon salt**	

1 Bring the water to a boil in a Dutch oven. Add the lentils and return to a boil. Reduce the heat; cover and simmer until softened, 20 minutes. Stir in the rice, cumin, allspice, salt, and cayenne. Cover and cook until the rice is tender, 20 minutes. Remove the Dutch oven from the heat; stir in the carrots and cilantro. Cover and let stand until the carrots are wilted, 5 minutes.

2 Meanwhile, heat the oil in a large nonstick skillet over medium-high heat. Add the onions and cook, stirring frequently, until browned, about 10 minutes.

3 Transfer 2 cups of the lentils and rice and ¼ cup of the onions to a container and let cool. Cover and refrigerate up to 3 days for later use in Lentil Soup with Yogurt-Cilantro Topping, opposite. Transfer the remaining 6 cups of lentils and rice to a platter and serve topped with the remaining onions.

PER SERVING (1½ cups lentils and rice with 3 tablespoons onions): 427 Cal, 4 g Fat, 1 g Sat Fat, 0 g Trans Fat, 0 mg Chol, 142 mg Sod, 78 g Carb, 14 g Fib, 22 g Prot, 84 mg Calc. **POINTS** value: **8.**

...then this! ## Lentil Soup with Yogurt-Cilantro Topping

prep 10 MIN • cook 10 MIN • serves 4

2   cups reserved cooked lentils and rice and ¼ cup reserved cooked onions from Middle Eastern-Style Lentils and Rice (opposite)

1   (14½-ounce) can petite diced tomatoes

2   cups low-sodium vegetable broth

¼   teaspoon salt

¼   teaspoon black pepper

1   cup fat-free plain yogurt

¼   cup fresh cilantro leaves

2   scallions, thinly sliced

1 Mix the lentils and rice, onions, tomatoes, broth, salt, and pepper in a large saucepan. Bring to a boil over medium-high heat, stirring occasionally.

2 Meanwhile, mix the yogurt, cilantro, and scallions in a small bowl. Divide the soup among 4 bowls. Serve topped with the yogurt mixture.

PER SERVING (2 cups with about 2 tablespoons yogurt mixture): 203 Cal, 2 g Fat, 0 g Sat Fat, 0 g Trans Fat, 1 mg Chol, 522 mg Sod, 37 g Carb, 6 g Fib, 12 g Prot, 192 mg Calc. *POINTS* value: *3.*

make this... Polenta with Tomato Sauce

prep 10 MIN • cook 20 MIN • serves 4 PLUS LEFTOVERS

1	tablespoon olive oil	⅛	teaspoon red pepper flakes
1	small red onion, finely chopped	¼	cup chopped fresh flat-leaf parsley
1	garlic clove, minced	4	cups low-sodium vegetable broth
½	teaspoon dried basil, crumbled	1½	cups instant polenta
2	(14½-ounce) cans petite diced tomatoes	½	cup shredded part-skim mozzarella cheese
¼	teaspoon salt		

1 Heat the oil in a large saucepan over medium heat. Add the onion and cook, stirring occasionally, until softened, 4 minutes. Add the garlic and basil; cook, stirring constantly, until fragrant, 1 minute. Add the tomatoes, salt, and pepper flakes; bring to a boil, stirring occasionally. Reduce the heat and simmer, stirring occasionally, until slightly thickened, 15 minutes. Stir in the parsley. Transfer 1 cup of the tomato mixture to a container and let cool. Cover and refrigerate up to 4 days for later use in Savory Baked Eggs, opposite.

2 Meanwhile, bring the broth to a boil in a medium saucepan. Slowly pour in the polenta in a thin, steady stream, beating constantly with a whisk. Reduce the heat and cook, whisking constantly, until thick and creamy, 3–5 minutes.

3 Spoon the polenta into a large bowl. Top with the remaining 2 cups of tomato sauce and sprinkle with the cheese.

PER SERVING (1 cup polenta, ½ cup tomato sauce, and 2 tablespoons cheese): 224 Cal, 5 g Fat, 2 g Sat Fat, 0 g Trans Fat, 9 mg Chol, 1,056 mg Sod, 40 g Carb, 4 g Fib, 8 g Prot, 306 mg Calc. *POINTS* value: *4.*

...then this! Savory Baked Eggs

prep 5 MIN • bake 25 MIN • serves 4

1   **cup reserved cooked tomato sauce from Polenta with Tomato Sauce (opposite)**

4   **large eggs**

⅛   **teaspoon salt**

⅛   **teaspoon black pepper**

2   **tablespoons chopped fresh chives**

1 Preheat the oven to 350°F. Spray 4 (6-ounce) custard cups or ramekins with nonstick spray.

2 Divide the tomato sauce evenly among the prepared cups. Let the sauce come to room temperature, 15 minutes.

3 Carefully break 1 egg into each cup; sprinkle with the salt and pepper. Place the cups on a baking sheet and bake until the eggs are just set, 25–30 minutes. Sprinkle with the chives.

PER SERVING (1 baked egg): 103 Cal, 7 g Fat, 2 g Sat Fat, 0 g Trans Fat, 212 mg Chol, 504 mg Sod, 4 g Carb, 1 g Fib, 7 g Prot, 54 mg Calc. **POINTS** value: **2.**

Cheese Ravioli with Roasted Cauliflower

prep 15 MIN · roast/cook 40 MIN · serves 4 PLUS LEFTOVERS

1   large cauliflower, trimmed and cut into florets
    (8 cups)

1   tablespoon olive oil

¼   teaspoon black pepper

2   (9-ounce) packages low-fat cheese ravioli

1   pint cherry tomatoes, halved

1   garlic clove, minced

¾   teaspoon salt

½   teaspoon fresh thyme leaves
    or ¼ teaspoon dried

1 Preheat the oven to 450°F. Spray a large rimmed baking sheet with nonstick spray. Toss the cauliflower, oil, and pepper in a large bowl. Spread on the prepared baking sheet. Roast until the cauliflower is fork-tender, 40 minutes, stirring 3 times during cooking.

2 Meanwhile, cook the ravioli according to the package directions, omitting the oil and salt if desired.

3 Transfer the cauliflower to a medium bowl; stir in the tomatoes, garlic, salt, and thyme. Transfer 2 cups of the cauliflower mixture to a container and let cool. Cover and refrigerate up to 2 days for later use in Cauliflower Frittata, opposite. Drain the ravioli and toss with the remaining 2 cups of cauliflower mixture.

PER SERVING (generous 1 cup): 376 Cal, 8 g Fat, 3 g Sat Fat, 0 g Trans Fat, 56 mg Chol, 830 mg Sod, 59 g Carb, 6 g Fib, 19 g Prot, 154 mg Calc. **POINTS** value: **7.**

Cauliflower Frittata

prep 10 MIN · cook/bake 30 MIN · serves 4

2 teaspoons olive oil	¼ teaspoon salt
2 small red onions, thinly sliced	Pinch black pepper
2 cups reserved cooked cauliflower mixture from Cheese Ravioli with Roasted Cauliflower (opposite)	1 (16-ounce) carton fat-free egg substitute

1 Preheat the oven to 375°F.

2 Heat the oil in an 8-inch ovenproof nonstick skillet over medium-high heat. Add the onions and cook, stirring occasionally, until softened, 5 minutes. Stir in the cauliflower, salt, and pepper; cook, stirring occasionally, until heated through, 2 minutes.

3 Remove the skillet from the heat and stir in the egg substitute. Set the skillet over medium-low heat and cook until the frittata is almost set around the edges, 3 minutes. Place the skillet in the oven and bake just until set in the center, 18 minutes. Invert onto a plate and cut into 4 wedges.

PER SERVING (1 wedge): 143 Cal, 4 g Fat, 1 g Sat Fat, 0 g Trans Fat, 0 mg Chol, 638 mg Sod, 13 g Carb, 5 g Fib, 15 g Prot, 240 mg Calc. **POINTS** value: **2.**

Hungarian Pepper Stew with Noodles

prep 15 MIN • cook 30 MIN • serves 4 PLUS LEFTOVERS

4 cups whole-grain yolk-free wide noodles	½ teaspoon salt
1 tablespoon olive oil	¼ teaspoon black pepper
2 red onions, thinly sliced	3 assorted-color bell peppers, thinly sliced
1 garlic clove, minced	1 (14½-ounce) can petite diced tomatoes
1½ teaspoons paprika	½ cup water
½ teaspoon dried thyme	½ cup chopped fresh flat-leaf parsley

1 Cook the noodles according to the package directions, omitting the salt if desired.

2 Heat the oil in a large skillet over medium heat. Add the onions and cook, stirring occasionally, until softened, 10 minutes. Add the garlic, paprika, thyme, salt, and black pepper; cook, stirring constantly, until fragrant, 1 minute. Increase the heat and add the bell peppers, tomatoes, and water; cover and cook, stirring frequently, until the bell peppers are softened, 20 minutes. Stir in the parsley.

3 Transfer 1 cup of the bell pepper mixture to a container and let cool. Cover and refrigerate up to 3 days for later use in Bell Pepper Tabbouleh Salad, opposite. Drain the noodles and transfer to a large bowl. Top with the remaining 2 cups of bell pepper mixture.

PER SERVING (½ cup bell pepper mixture with 1 cup noodles): 251 Cal, 4 g Fat, 1 g Sat Fat, 0 g Trans Fat, 0 mg Chol, 472 mg Sod, 52 g Carb, 9 g Fib, 10 g Prot, 72 mg Calc. **POINTS** value: **5.**

Bell Pepper Tabbouleh Salad

prep 10 MIN • cook 5 MIN • serves 4

1⅓ cups water

1 cup bulgur

1 cup reserved cooked bell pepper mixture from Hungarian Pepper Stew with Noodles (opposite)

2 teaspoons balsamic vinegar

¼ teaspoon salt

¼ teaspoon black pepper

4 cups mixed salad greens

1 Bring the water to a boil in a small saucepan. Stir in the bulgur; remove the pan from the heat. Cover and let stand until the water is absorbed and the bulgur is tender, about 25 minutes.

2 Meanwhile, coarsely chop the bell pepper mixture. Fluff the bulgur with a fork and transfer to a large bowl. Add the bell pepper mixture, vinegar, salt, and pepper; mix well. Place the greens on a platter and top with the bulgur mixture.

PER SERVING (1 cup salad greens with ⅔ cup bulgur mixture): 165 Cal, 2 g Fat, 0 g Sat Fat, 0 g Trans Fat, 0 mg Chol, 323 mg Sod, 34 g Carb, 9 g Fib, 6 g Prot, 65 mg Calc. *POINTS* value: *3.*

◆ Filling Extra

If you wish, add a 15-ounce can drained chickpeas to the salad in step 2. This will increase the per-serving *POINTS* value by *1.*

make this... # Gnocchi with Tomato and Parmesan

prep 15 MIN • bake/cook 30 MIN • serves 4 PLUS LEFTOVERS

2 pints grape tomatoes, halved	**1** tablespoon extra-virgin olive oil
1 (17.5-ounce) package potato gnocchi	**½** teaspoon salt
	⅛ teaspoon black pepper
12 fresh basil leaves, thinly sliced	**¼** cup shaved Parmesan cheese
1 garlic clove, minced	

1 Spray a large rimmed baking sheet with nonstick spray, place in the oven, and preheat the oven to 450°F. Spread the tomatoes on the prepared baking sheet and roast until softened, 30 minutes, stirring every 10 minutes.

2 Meanwhile, cook the gnocchi according to the package directions, omitting the salt if desired.

3 Transfer the tomatoes to a large bowl; stir in the basil, garlic, oil, salt, and pepper. Transfer ¾ cup of the tomato mixture to a container and let cool. Cover and refrigerate up to 4 days for later use in Grape Tomato Clafouti, opposite. Drain the gnocchi and toss with the remaining 1 cup of tomato mixture. Sprinkle with the cheese.

PER SERVING (1 cup): 251 Cal, 4 g Fat, 1 g Sat Fat, 0 g Trans Fat, 5 mg Chol, 712 mg Sod, 47 g Carb, 3 g Fib, 7 g Prot, 96 mg Calc. **POINTS** value: **5.**

...then this!

Grape Tomato Clafouti

prep 10 MIN · bake 30 MIN · serves 4

¾ cup reserved cooked tomato mixture from
  Gnocchi with Tomato and Parmesan (opposite)

2 thinly sliced fresh basil leaves

1 (4-ounce) carton fat-free egg substitute

¾ cup fat-free sour cream

¼ cup fat-free milk

¼ cup all-purpose flour

¼ teaspoon salt

⅛ teaspoon black pepper

1 Preheat the oven to 375°F. Spray an 8-inch ovenproof nonstick skillet with nonstick spray.

2 Mix the tomatoes and basil in a small bowl; spread in the prepared skillet.

3 Whisk together the egg substitute, sour cream, milk, flour, salt, and pepper in a medium bowl. Pour the egg mixture over the tomato mixture and bake until the top is puffed and golden, 30–35 minutes. Cut into 4 wedges.

PER SERVING (1 wedge): 109 Cal, 2 g Fat, 0 g Sat Fat, 0 g Trans Fat, 4 mg Chol, 410 mg Sod, 17 g Carb, 1 g Fib, 6 g Prot, 137 mg Calc. POINTS value: 2.

make this... Roasted Corn Chowder

prep 20 MIN · roast/cook 35 MIN · serves 4 PLUS LEFTOVERS

2 (10-ounce) packages frozen corn kernels, thawed	8 tiny red potatoes (6 ounces), cut into quarters
1 tablespoon olive oil	¼ teaspoon salt
1 red onion, finely chopped	⅛ teaspoon black pepper
2 celery stalks with leaves, thinly sliced	½ cup chopped fresh flat-leaf parsley
1 tablespoon all-purpose flour	½ cup grated Parmesan cheese
3 cups low-sodium vegetable broth	

1 Preheat the oven to 425°F. Spray a large rimmed baking sheet with nonstick spray.

2 Spread the corn on the prepared baking sheet and roast until lightly browned, 25 minutes, stirring twice during cooking.

3 Meanwhile, heat the oil in a large saucepan over medium heat. Add the onion and cook, stirring occasionally, until softened, 5 minutes. Add the celery and cook, stirring occasionally, until softened, 3 minutes. Stir in the flour and cook, stirring constantly, 1 minute.

4 Gradually stir in the broth until blended. Stir in the corn, potatoes, salt, and pepper; bring to a boil. Reduce the heat and simmer, stirring occasionally, until the potatoes are fork-tender, 15 minutes. Let cool 5 minutes. Puree 2 cups of the chowder in a blender or food processor. Transfer 1 cup of the puree to a container and let cool. Cover and refrigerate up to 2 days for later use in Skillet Corn and Bean Chilaquiles, opposite. Stir the remaining 1 cup of puree and the parsley into the chowder. Divide the soup among 4 bowls and sprinkle with the cheese.

PER SERVING (1½ cups with 2 tablespoons cheese): 226 Cal, 7 g Fat, 3 g Sat Fat, 0 g Trans Fat, 9 mg Chol, 508 mg Sod, 36 g Carb, 5 g Fib, 9 g Prot, 177 mg Calc. **POINTS** value: **4.**

Skillet Corn and Bean Chilaquiles

prep 20 MIN • bake/cook 25 MIN • serves 4

6   (6-inch) corn tortillas

6   plum tomatoes, seeded and chopped

2   red onions, chopped

2   jalapeño peppers, seeded and chopped

2   garlic cloves, peeled

1   cup reserved cooked puree from Roasted Corn Chowder (opposite)

1   (15½-ounce) can kidney beans, rinsed and drained

¼   cup + 2 tablespoons fresh cilantro leaves

½   cup fat-free sour cream

1 Preheat the oven to 375°F.

2 Cut each tortilla into 8 wedges. Place on a large baking sheet in a single layer and bake until crisp, 20 minutes.

3 Meanwhile, combine the tomatoes, onions, jalapeños, and garlic in a large skillet. Cook over medium heat, stirring occasionally, until the vegetables are softened, 12 minutes. Let the mixture cool 5 minutes. Puree, in batches if necessary, in a blender or food processor. Return the mixture to the skillet. Add the corn puree, tortillas, and beans; cook over medium heat, stirring frequently, until the tortillas are softened, 10 minutes. Stir in ¼ cup of the cilantro. Divide the mixture among 4 bowls. Top with the sour cream and the remaining 2 tablespoons of cilantro.

PER SERVING (1 cup with 2 tablespoons sour cream): 265 Cal, 2 g Fat, 0 g Sat Fat, 0 g Trans Fat, 3 mg Chol, 297 mg Sod, 53 g Carb, 10 g Fib, 12 g Prot, 122 mg Calc. *POINTS* value: **5.**

In the Kitchen

If you're making Roasted Corn Chowder in the summer, substitute fresh corn for the frozen. To remove the kernels, stand each ear on its stem end and use a sharp knife to cut away three or four rows at a time. You will need 5 ears of corn to equal two 10-ounce packages of frozen corn.

Butternut Squash Soup

prep 20 MIN · cook 25 MIN · serves 4 PLUS LEFTOVERS

1	tablespoon olive oil	1	celery stalk with leaves, finely chopped
2	medium red onions, thinly sliced	1½	teaspoons fresh thyme leaves or
1	garlic clove, minced		¾ teaspoon dried
4	cups low-sodium vegetable broth	¾	teaspoon salt
3	cups peeled and diced butternut squash	⅛	teaspoon black pepper
1	parsnip, peeled and diced	2	tablespoons chopped fresh flat-leaf parsley

1 Heat the oil in a large saucepan over medium heat. Add the onions and cook, stirring occasionally, until softened, 6 minutes. Add the garlic and cook, stirring constantly, until fragrant, 1 minute. Stir in the broth, squash, parsnip, celery, thyme, salt, and pepper; bring to a boil. Reduce the heat; cover and simmer, stirring occasionally, until the squash is fork-tender, 15 minutes.

2 Transfer 2 cups of the soup to a container and let cool. Cover and refrigerate up to 4 days for later use in Vegetable-Barley Risotto, opposite. Divide the remaining 6 cups of soup among 4 bowls and serve sprinkled with the parsley.

PER SERVING (1½ cups): 91 Cal, 3 g Fat, 0 g Sat Fat, 0 g Trans Fat, 0 mg Chol, 542 mg Sod, 17 g Carb, 3 g Fib, 2 g Prot, 56 mg Calc. **POINTS** value: *1*.

◆ Filling Extra

Serve the Butternut Squash Soup with a satisfying salad: Cook tempeh in a nonstick skillet sprayed with nonstick spray until heated through (3 ounces tempeh for each serving will increase the **POINTS** value by *4*). Serve the tempeh on a bed of mixed salad greens.

...then this! # Vegetable-Barley Risotto

prep 10 MIN · cook 20 MIN · serves 4

2	cups reserved cooked Butternut Squash Soup (opposite)
1	(14½-ounce) can petite diced tomatoes
¾	cup barley
½	cup water

¼	teaspoon salt
⅛	teaspoon black pepper
¼	cup grated Parmesan cheese
¼	cup chopped fresh flat-leaf parsley

1 Mix the soup, tomatoes, barley, water, salt, and pepper in a large saucepan; bring to a boil. Reduce the heat; cook, covered, stirring occasionally, until the barley is almost cooked through, 20 minutes.

2 Uncover and cook, stirring frequently, until the barley is tender, 5 minutes. Stir in the cheese and parsley.

PER SERVING (generous 1 cup): 209 Cal, 3 g Fat, 1 g Sat Fat, 0 g Trans Fat, 5 mg Chol, 594 mg Sod, 39 g Carb, 8 g Fib, 8 g Prot, 152 mg Calc. *POINTS* value: **4.**

Roasted Beet and Goat Cheese Salad with Mint

prep 20 MIN • roast 1 HR 15 MIN • serves 4 PLUS LEFTOVERS

8   small beets, trimmed (1¼ pounds)

Juice of ½ lemon

1   tablespoon extra-virgin olive oil

1   garlic clove, minced

½   teaspoon salt

¼   teaspoon cumin seeds, crushed

¼   teaspoon black pepper

8   cups baby spinach leaves

1   cup fresh mint leaves

¼   cup crumbled low-fat goat cheese

1 Preheat the oven to 425°F. Place the beets on the center of a double layer of foil, about 20 inches long. Make a packet by bringing 2 sides of the foil up to meet in the center, and pressing the edges together to make 2 (½-inch) folds. Then fold the edges together into 2 (½-inch) folds. Crimp the edges together to seal tightly. Place the packet on a baking sheet and roast until the beets are fork-tender, 1 hour 15 minutes. Let stand in the packet until cool enough to handle, 20 minutes. Peel the beets and dice. Transfer 2 cups of the beets to a container and let cool. Cover and refrigerate up to 4 days for later use in Roasted Beet and White Bean Soup, opposite.

2 Meanwhile, to make the dressing, combine the lemon juice, oil, garlic, salt, cumin seeds, and pepper in a large bowl; whisk until blended.

3 Add the remaining ½ cup of beets, the spinach, and mint to the dressing; toss to coat. Sprinkle with the cheese and serve.

PER SERVING (1½ cups salad with 1 tablespoon cheese): 123 Cal, 9 g Fat, 4 g Sat Fat, 0 g Trans Fat, 9 mg Chol, 523 mg Sod, 7 g Carb, 2 g Fib, 6 g Prot, 94 mg Calc. **POINTS** value: **3.**

Roasted Beet and White Bean Soup

prep 15 MIN • cook 15 MIN • serves 4

1   tablespoon olive oil

2   small red onions, thinly sliced

1   carrot, shredded

1   garlic clove, minced

3   cups low-sodium vegetable broth

1   (15½-ounce) can white beans

1   (14½-ounce) can petite diced tomatoes

½   teaspoon salt

⅛   teaspoon black pepper

2   cups reserved cooked beets from Roasted Beet and Goat Cheese Salad with Mint (opposite)

¼   cup plain fat-free yogurt

1 Heat the oil in a large saucepan over medium heat. Add the onions and carrot; cook, stirring occasionally, until the vegetables soften, 5 minutes. Add the garlic and cook, stirring frequently, until fragrant, 1 minute. Stir in the broth, beans, tomatoes, salt, and pepper; bring to a boil.

2 Coarsely chop the beets; add to the soup and cook until heated through, 1 minute. Divide the soup among 4 bowls. Serve topped with the yogurt.

PER SERVING (scant 2 cups with 1 tablespoon yogurt): 222 Cal, 4 g Fat, 1 g Sat Fat, 0 g Trans Fat, 0 mg Chol, 949 mg Sod, 39 g Carb, 8 g Fib, 11 g Prot, 161 mg Calc. **POINTS** value: **4.**

In the Kitchen

If you've only had beets from a can, these recipes using fresh beets will be a delicious discovery. Once the baked beets are cool for making Roasted Beet and Goat Cheese Salad with Mint, you can slip the skins off with your hands (be sure to wear gloves to keep your hands from staining).

ASIAN-STYLE GRILLED
FLANK STEAK, PAGE 12

Dry and Liquid Measurement Equivalents

If you are converting the recipes in this book to metric measurements, use the following chart as a guide.

TEASPOONS	TABLESPOONS	CUPS	FLUID OUNCES
3 teaspoons	1 tablespoon		½ fluid ounce
6 teaspoons	2 tablespoons	⅛ cup	1 fluid ounce
8 teaspoons	2 tablespoons plus 2 teaspoons	⅙ cup	
12 teaspoons	4 tablespoons	¼ cup	2 fluid ounces
15 teaspoons	5 tablespoons	⅓ cup minus 1 teaspoon	
16 teaspoons	5 tablespoons plus 1 teaspoon	⅓ cup	
18 teaspoons	6 tablespoons	¼ cup plus 2 tablespoons	3 fluid ounces
24 teaspoons	8 tablespoons	½ cup	4 fluid ounces
30 teaspoons	10 tablespoons	½ cup plus 2 tablespoons	5 fluid ounces
32 teaspoons	10 tablespoons plus 2 teaspoons	⅔ cup	
36 teaspoons	12 tablespoons	¾ cup	6 fluid ounces
42 teaspoons	14 tablespoons	1 cup minus 2 tablespoons	7 fluid ounces
45 teaspoons	15 tablespoons	1 cup minus 1 tablespoon	
48 teaspoons	16 tablespoons	1 cup	8 fluid ounces

VOLUME	
¼ teaspoon	1 milliliter
½ teaspoon	2 milliliters
1 teaspoon	5 milliliters
1 tablespoon	15 milliliters
2 tablespoons	30 milliliters
3 tablespoons	45 milliliters
¼ cup	60 milliliters
⅓ cup	80 milliliters
½ cup	120 milliliters
⅔ cup	160 milliliters
¾ cup	175 milliliters
1 cup	240 milliliters
1 quart	950 milliliters

LENGTH	
1 inch	25 millimeters
1 inch	2.5 centimeters

OVEN TEMPERATURE			
250°F	120°C	400°F	200°C
275°F	140°C	425°F	220°C
300°F	150°C	450°F	230°C
325°F	160°C	475°F	250°C
350°F	180°C	500°F	260°C
375°F	190°C	525°F	270°C

WEIGHT	
1 ounce	30 grams
¼ pound	120 grams
½ pound	240 grams
1 pound	480 grams

NOTE: Measurement of less than ⅛ teaspoon is considered a dash or a pinch. Metric volume measurements are approximate.

Recipe Index

A

Apples

Chicken Waldorf Salad, *55*

Cornish Hens with, *86*

Ham and Apple Slaw, 43

Apricot-Glazed Chicken, 58

Argentinean-Style Chicken, 62

Artichokes

Chicken with Olives and, *60*

Asian-Style Burgers, *81*

Asian-Style Grilled Flank Steak, *12*

Asian-Style Pork Roast, 126

Asparagus

Chicken and Risotto, 57

Linguine and Ricotta with, *114*

Negamaki with Ginger Dipping Sauce, *13*

B

Baked Pasta and Meatballs, 106

Baked Pasta e Fagioli, 113

Balsamic Sausage and Peppers, 40

Balsamic Vegetable and Tofu Salad, 149

BBQ Turkey, *140*

Beans

Baked Pasta e Fagioli, 113

and Beef Sloppy Joes, 23

Cajun Nachos, 159

Cannellini and Swiss Chard with Ricotta and, 154

Chickpea-Vegetable Salad, 153

Double Soy Soup, *151*

Easy Cassoulet, *129*

Easy Chickpea Curry, 152

Edamame-Zucchini Sauté, 148

Greek Vegetable-Noodle Soup, 117

Lemon-Honey Carrots and, 160

Lemony Pork and Lentil Salad, 37

Lentil Soup with Yogurt-Cilantro Topping, 163

Mexicali Pork Stew, 130

Middle Eastern-Style Lentils and Rice, 162

Raspberry Wild Rice and Bean Salad, 161

Roasted Beet and White Bean Soup, 177

Sausage and Lentils, 82

Sesame Edamame Salad, *150*

Skillet Corn Chilaquiles and, 173

Slow-Cooker Beef Chili, 122

Smoky Bean and Ham Soup, *128*

Spiced Three-Bean Stew, 158

Stuffed Bell Peppers with Tomato-Basil Sauce, 147

Sweet Potato and Chickpea Salad, *156*

Tex-Mex Taco Salad, 123

Tuscan Pasta and Bean Salad with Tuna, *111*

Veggie Tofu Burgers, 146

Beef

Asian-Style Grilled Flank Steak, *12*

and Bean Sloppy Joes, 23

Burgundy Stew, 16

Chimichurri Pepper Steak, *18*

Corned Beef Hash, 21

Easy Beef Curry, 15

French Dip Sandwiches, 11

Hoisin Burgers, 24

Hoisin Noodles with Broccoli and, 94

Italian-Style Pot Roast, *120*

Italian Wedding Soup, *27*

Korean, in Lettuce Cups, 25

Lebanese Pita Pizzas, 29

Negamaki with Ginger Dipping Sauce, *13*

Noodle Soup Bowl, 95

Old-Fashioned Meatloaf, *26*

Philly Cheese Steak Sandwiches, *121*

Pressure-Cooker Corned Beef, 20

Savory Slow-Cooker Meatloaf, 124

Slow-Cooker Chili, 122

Smoky Beef Tacos, 22

Speedy Beef Fajitas, *19*

Spiced Steak with Onions and Peppers, 10

Spicy Taco Soup, 97

Stroganoff, 17

Tandoori Beef Kebabs, 14

Tex-Mex Chili Pasta, 96

Tex-Mex Taco Salad, 123

in Tomato-Ginger Sauce, 28

Beef and Bean Sloppy Joes, 23

Beef Burgundy Stew, 16

Beef in Tomato-Ginger Sauce, 28

Beef-Noodle Soup Bowl, 95

Beef Stroganoff, 17

Beets

Goat Cheese Salad with Mint and Roasted, 176

White Bean Soup and Roasted, 177

Bell Pepper Tabbouleh Salad, 169

Bok Choy

Pork Noodle Bowl and, 31

Braised Chicken and Couscous, 100

Broccoli

Hoisin Noodles with Beef and, 94

Penne with Sausage and, *110*

Buffalo Chicken Salad, 133

Burgers

Asian-Style, *81*

Hoisin, 24

Veggie Tofu, 146

Butternut Squash Soup, 174

C

Cajun Bean Nachos, 159

Cannellini Beans and Swiss Chard with Ricotta, 154

Caribbean Cornish Hen and Sweet Potato Salad, *87*

Carrots

Lemon-Honey Beans and, 160

Casseroles

Baked Pasta and Meatballs, 106

Baked Pasta e Fagioli, 113

Chicken and Penne Casserole, 71

Lamb-Noodle Casserole, 47

Mexican Pork and Veggie Bake, 33

Pasta "Pizza", *115*

Cauliflower

Cheese Ravioli with Roasted, 166

Frittata, 167

Cauliflower Frittata, 167

Cheese

Cannellini Beans and Swiss Chard with Ricotta, 154

Chicken Mac 'n,' 102

Gnocchi with Tomato and Parmesan, *170*

Linguine with Asparagus and Ricotta, *114*

Mac 'n' Cheese Cakes with Greens and Ham, 103

Philly Cheese Steak Sandwiches, *121*

Ravioli Bolognese, *104*

Ravioli Minestrone, *105*

Roasted Beet and Goat Cheese Salad with Mint, 176

Roasted Vegetable-Feta Pasta, 116

Cheese Ravioli with Roasted Cauliflower, 166

Cherries

Duck with Brandied, 88

Chicken

Apricot-Glazed, 58

Argentinean-Style Chicken, 62

Braised, and Couscous, 100

Buffalo Salad, 133

Caribbean Cornish Hen and Sweet Potato Salad, *87*

Chicken and Asparagus Risotto, 57

Chicken Waldorf Salad, *55*

Chili Con Pollo, 70

Cornish Hens with Apples, *86*

Couscous Salad, 101

Croquettes with Marinara Sauce, *61*

Cubano Panini, 59

Easy Cassoulet, *129*

Egg Foo Yung, 69

Farfalle with Sausage, Fennel, and Peppers, *75*

Fried Rice, 137

Mac 'n' Cheese, 102

Mango-Glazed Drumsticks, 68

Marengo, 56

Middle-Eastern, *66*

Moroccan Meatballs with Couscous, 72

with Olives and Artichokes, *60*

and Penne Casserole, 71

Roast with Lemon and Oregano, *54*

Salsa Chicken Wraps, *135*

Samosas with Mango Chutney, *67*

Sausage and Polenta Ragoût, *74*

and Shrimp Tortilla Soup, 63

Spaghetti Primavera with Sausage, 108

Spanish Rice and, *134*

Spicy Meatball Pitas with Yogurt Sauce, 73

Spicy Stew, 136

Thai Salad, 65

Tropical, 132

Vietnamese Chicken Curry, 64

Chicken and Asparagus Risotto, 57

Chicken and Penne Casserole, 71

Chicken and Shrimp Tortilla Soup, 63

Chicken-Couscous Salad, 101

Chicken Croquettes with Marinara Sauce, *61*

Chicken Cubano Panini, 59

Chicken Egg Foo Yung, 69

Chicken Fried Rice, 137

Chicken Mac 'n' Cheese, 102

Chicken Marengo, 56

Chicken Samosas with Mango Chutney, *67*

Chicken Waldorf Salad, *55*

Chicken with Olives and Artichokes, *60*

Chickpea-Vegetable Salad, 153

Chili

Con Pollo, 70

Double Chili Pork Roast, 30

Slow-Cooker Beef, 122

Tex-Mex Pasta, 96

Chili Con Pollo, 70

Chimichurri Pepper Steak, *18*

Chinese Pork and Noodles, *98*

Chipotle Roast Pork, 32

Chutney

Chicken Samosas with Mango, *67*

Ham with Fresh Peach, 42

Coconut

Thai Soup, *99*

Corn

Roasted Corn Chowder, 172

Rotini with Shrimp and, 112

Savory Duck and Corn Salad, 89

Skillet Bean Chilaquiles and, 173

Corned Beef Hash, 21

Cornish Hens

with Apples, *86*

Caribbean and Sweet Potato Salad, *87*

Jamaican Sandwiches with Mango Mayonnaise, 85

Spicy, with Mango Sauce, 84

Cornish Hens with Apples, *86*

Couscous

Braised Chicken and, 100

Chicken Salad and, 101

Moroccan Meatballs with, 72

Crunchy Turkey Caesar Salad, 79

Curry

Easy Beef, 15

Easy Chickpea, 152

Vietnamese Chicken, 64

D

Double Chili Pork Roast, 30

Double Soy Soup, *151*

Duck

Duck with Brandied Cherries, 88

Grilled Duck with Spicy Grapefruit Salsa, 90

Hash, 91

Savory Duck and Corn Salad, 89

Duck Hash, 91

Duck with Brandied Cherries, 88

Dumplings

Wasabi Soup and, *80*

E

East-West Turkey Wraps, 77

Easy Beef Curry, 15

Easy Cassoulet, *129*

Easy Chickpea Curry, 152

Edamame-Zucchini Sauté, 148

Eggs

Cauliflower Frittata, 167

Chicken Egg Foo Yung, 69

Duck Hash, 91

Grape Tomato Clafouti, *171*

Savory Baked, *165*

Spaghetti and Spinach Frittata, 109

Ethnic Cuisine

Argentinean-Style Chicken, 62

Asian-Style Burgers, *81*

Asian-Style Grilled Flank Steak, *12*

Asian-Style Pork Roast, 126

Baked Pasta e Fagioli, 113

Beef Stroganoff, 17

Cajun Bean Nachos, 159

Caribbean Cornish Hen and Sweet Potato Salad, *87*

Chicken Cubano Panini, 59

Chicken Egg Foo Yung, 69

Chicken Marengo, 56

Chicken Samosas with Mango Chutney, *67*

Chili Con Pollo, 70

Chimichurri Pepper Steak, *18*

Chinese Pork and Noodles, *98*

East-West Turkey Wraps, 77

French Dip Sandwiches, 11

Gnocchi with Tomato and Parmesan, *170*

Grape Tomato Clafouti, *171*

Greek Vegetable-Noodle Soup, 117

Hoisin Burgers, 24

Hoisin Noodles with Beef and Broccoli, 94

Hunan Pork and Peppers, 127

Hungarian Pepper Stew with Noodles, 168

Italian-Style Pot Roast, *120*

Italian Wedding Soup, *27*

Jamaican Sandwiches with Mango Mayonnaise, 85

Korean Beef in Lettuce Cups, 25

Lamb Tagine with Apricots, *45*

Lebanese Pita Pizzas, 29

Mexicali Pork Stew, 130

Mexican Pork and Veggie Bake, 33

Middle-Eastern Chicken, *66*

Middle Eastern-Style Lentils and Rice, 162

Moroccan Meatballs with Couscous, 72

Negamaki with Ginger Dipping Sauce, *13*

Pork and Bok Choy Noodle Bowl, 31

Pork and Rice Burritos, 131

Pork Tostadas, *35*

Ravioli Bolognese, *104*

Ravioli Minestrone, *105*

Salsa Verde Pork Stew, *34*

Saltimbocca Fennel and Orange Salad, 51

Samosas with Mango Chutney, *67*

Sicilian Meatball Soup, 107

Skillet Corn and Bean Chilaquiles, 173

Spaghetti Primavera with Sausage, 108

Spanish Chicken and Rice, *134*

Tandoori Beef Kabobs, 14

Tex-Mex Chili Pasta, 96

Tex-Mex Taco Salad, 123

Thai Chicken Salad, 65

Thai Coconut Soup, *99*

Thai Tofu and Vegetable Stir-Fry, *145*

Turkey Kiev Rolls, 78

Turkey Tonnato, 139

Tuscan Braised Turkey, 138

Tuscan Pasta and Bean Salad with Tuna, *111*

Veal Stew Marsala, 48

Vietnamese Chicken Curry, 64

Wasabi Dumpling Soup, *80*

Veal Saltimbocca, 50

F

Fajitas

   Speedy Beef, *19*

Farfalle with Sausage, Fennel, and Peppers, *75*

Fennel

   Farfalle with Sausage and Peppers, *75*

   Orange-Glazed Pork Chops with, 36

   Saltimbocca Fennel and Orange Salad, 51

French Dip Sandwiches, 11

Fruit

   Duck with Brandied Cherries, 88

   Grilled Duck with Spicy Grapefruit Salsa, 90

   Ham and Apple Slaw, 43

   Ham with Fresh Peach Chutney, 42

   Lamb Tagine with Apricots, *45*

G

Ginger

   Beef in Tomato-Ginger Sauce, 28

Gnocchi with Tomato and Parmesan, *170*

Grains

   Bell Pepper Tabbouleh Salad, 169

   Quinoa with Swiss Chard and Almonds, 155

   Roast Lamb with Bulgur and Mint Pesto, *44*

   Vegetable-Barley Risotto, 175

Grape Tomato Clafouti, *171*

Greek Vegetable-Noodle Soup, 117

Grilled Duck with Spicy Grapefruit Salsa, 90

H

Ham and Apple Slaw, 43

Ham with Fresh Peach Chutney, 42

Hash

   Corned Beef, 21

   Duck, 91

Hoisin Burgers, 24

Hoisin Noodles with Beef and Broccoli, 94

Hunan Pork and Peppers, 127

Hungarian Pepper Stew with Noodles, 168

I

Italian-Style Pot Roast, *120*

Italian Wedding Soup, *27*

J

Jamaican Sandwiches with Mango Mayonnaise, 85

K

Korean Beef in Lettuce Cups, 25

L

Lamb

   and Noodle Casserole, 47

   Roast, with Bulgur and Mint Pesto, *44*

   Tagine with Apricots, *45*

   in Tomato-Ginger Sauce, 28

   and Vegetable Stew, 46

Lamb and Vegetable Stew, 46

Lamb-Noodle Casserole, 47

Lamb Tagine with Apricots, *45*

Lebanese Pita Pizzas, 29

Lemon-Honey Beans and Carrots, 160

Lemons

Lemon-Honey Beans and Carrots, 160

Lemony Pork and Lentil Salad, 37

Lemony Tofu Caesar Salad, *144*

Roast Chicken with Lemon and Oregano, *54*

Lemony Pork and Lentil Salad, 37

Lemony Tofu Caesar Salad, *144*

Lentil Soup with Yogurt-Cilantro Topping, 163

Linguine with Asparagus and Ricotta, *114*

M

Mac 'n' Cheese Cakes with Greens and Ham, 103

Mango

Chicken Samosas with Chutney, *67*

Glazed Drumsticks, 68

Jamaican Sandwiches with Mayonnaise, 85

Spicy Cornish Hens with Sauce, 84

Mango-Glazed Drumsticks, 68

Meatballs

Baked Pasta and, 106

Moroccan with Couscous, 72

Spaghetti and, 125

Spicy Meatball Pitas with Yogurt Sauce, 73

Meatloaf

Old-Fashioned, *26*

Savory Slow-Cooker, 124

Mexicali Pork Stew, 130

Mexican Pork and Veggie Bake, 33

Middle-Eastern Chicken, *66*

Middle Eastern-Style Lentils and Rice, 162

Mint

Roasted Beet and Goat Cheese Salad with, 176

Roast Lamb with Bulgur and Mint Pesto, *44*

Miso-Glazed Pork, *38*

Moroccan Meatballs with Couscous, 72

N

Negamaki with Ginger Dipping Sauce, *13*

Nuts

Chicken Waldorf Salad, *55*

Quinoa with Swiss Chard and Almonds, 155

O

Old-Fashioned Meatloaf, *26*

Olives

Chicken and Artichokes with, *60*

Onions

Spiced Steak with Peppers and, 10

Orange-Glazed Pork Chops with Fennel, 36

Orange Roast Turkey, 76

Oranges

Glazed Pork Chops with Fennel and, 36

Roast Turkey, 76

Oregano

Roast Chicken with Lemon and Oregano, *54*

P

Panini

Chicken Cubano, 59

Pasta

Baked, and Meatballs, 106

Baked, e Fagioli, 113

Beef-Noodle Soup Bowl, 95

Braised Chicken and Couscous, 100

Cheese Ravioli with Roasted Cauliflower, 166

Chicken and Penne Casserole, 71

Chicken-Couscous Salad, 101

Chicken Mac 'n' Cheese, 102

Chinese Pork and Noodles, *98*

Farfalle with Sausage, Fennel, and Peppers, *75*

Gnocchi with Tomato and Parmesan, *170*

Greek Vegetable-Noodle Soup, 117

Hoisin Noodles with Beef and Broccoli, 94

Hungarian Pepper Stew with Noodles, 168

Lamb-Noodle Casserole, 47

Linguine with Asparagus and Ricotta, *114*

Mac 'n' Cheese Cakes with Greens and Ham, 103

Moroccan Meatballs with Couscous, 72

Penne with Sausage and Broccoli, *110*

"Pizza", *115*

Pork and Bok Choy Noodle Bowl, 31

Ravioli Bolognese, *104*

Ravioli Minestrone, *105*

Roasted Vegetable-Feta, 116

Rotini with Shrimp and Corn, 112

Spaghetti and "Meatballs", 125

Spaghetti and Spinach Frittata, 109

Spaghetti Primavera with Sausage, 108

Tex-Mex Chili, 96

Thai Coconut Soup, *99*

Tuscan Pasta and Bean Salad with Tuna, *111*

Pasta "Pizza", *115*

Penne with Sausage and Broccoli, *110*

Peppers

Balsamic Sausage and, 40

Bell Pepper Tabbouleh Salad, 169

Chimichurri Pepper Steak, *18*

Farfalle with Sausage, Fennel, and, *75*

Hunan Pork and, 127

Hungarian Stew with Noodles, 168

Sausage Shepherd's Pie, 41

Spiced Steak with Onions and, 10

Stuffed Bell Peppers with Tomato-Basil Sauce, 147

Philly Cheese Steak Sandwiches, *121*

Pie

Chicken Samosas with Mango Chutney, *67*

Sausage Shepherd's, 41

Pitas

Spicy Meatball with Yogurt Sauce, 73

Sweet Potato Falafel Sandwiches, *157*

Pizza

Lebanese Pita Pizzas, 29

Pasta, *115*

Polenta

and Sausage Ragoût, *74*

with Tomato Sauce, *164*

Polenta with Tomato Sauce, *164*

Pork

Asian-Style Roast, 126

Balsamic Sausage and Peppers, 40

and Bok Choy Noodle Bowl, 31

Chinese Noodles and, *98*

Chipotle Roast, 32

Double Chili Pork Roast, 30

Easy Cassoulet, *129*

Fried Rice, *39*

Ham and Apple Slaw, 43

Ham with Fresh Peach Chutney, 42

Hunan Peppers and, 127

Lemony Pork and Lentil Salad, 37

Mac 'n' Cheese Cakes with Greens and Ham, 103

Mexicali Stew, 130

Mexican Pork and Veggie Bake, 33

Miso-Glazed, *38*

Old-Fashioned Meatloaf, *26*

Orange-Glazed Pork Chops with Fennel, 36

and Rice Burritos, 131

Salsa Verde Stew, *34*

Sausage Shepherd's Pie, 41

Smoky Bean and Ham Soup, *128*

Thai Coconut Soup, *99*

Tostadas, *35*

Veal Saltimbocca, 50

Pork and Bok Choy Noodle Bowl, 31

Pork and Rice Burritos, 131

Pork Fried Rice, *39*

Pork Tostadas, *35*

Potatoes

Caribbean Cornish Hen and Sweet Potato Salad, *87*

Smoky Sausage and Potato Salad, 83

Sweet Potato and Chickpea Salad, *156*

Sweet Potato Falafel Sandwiches, *157*

Pressure-Cooker Corned Beef, 20

Q

Quinoa with Swiss Chard and Almonds, 155

R

Raspberry Wild Rice and Bean Salad, 161

Ravioli Bolognese, *104*

Ravioli Minestrone, *105*

Rice

Chicken and Asparagus Risotto, 57

Chicken Croquettes with Marinara Sauce, *61*

Chicken Fried, 137

Middle Eastern-Style Lentils and Rice, 162

Pork Burritos and, 131

Pork Fried, *39*

Raspberry Wild Rice and Bean Salad, 161

Spanish Chicken and, *134*

Turkey and Shrimp Gumbo, *141*

Roast Chicken with Lemon and Oregano, *54*

Roasted Beet and Goat Cheese Salad with Mint, 176

Roasted Beet and White Bean Soup, 177

Roasted Corn Chowder, 172

Roasted Vegetable-Feta Pasta, 116

Roast Lamb with Bulgur and Mint Pesto, *44*

Rotini with Shrimp and Corn, 112

S

Salads

Balsamic Vegetable and Tofu, 149

Bell Pepper Tabbouleh Salad, 169

Buffalo Chicken, 133

Caribbean Cornish Hen and Sweet Potato, *87*

Chicken-Couscous, 101

Chicken Waldorf, *55*

Chickpea-Vegetable, 153

Crunchy Turkey Caesar, 79

Ham and Apple Slaw, 43

Korean Beef in Lettuce Cups, 25

Lemony Pork and Lentil, 37

Lemony Tofu Caesar, *144*

Raspberry Wild Rice and Bean, 161

Roasted Beet and Goat Cheese with Mint, 176

Saltimbocca Fennel and Orange Salad, 51

Savory Duck and Corn Salad, 89

Sesame Edamame, *150*

Smoky Sausage and Potato Salad, 83

Sweet Potato and Chickpea, *156*

Tex-Mex Taco, 123

Thai Chicken, 65

Tuscan Pasta and Bean Salad with Tuna, *111*

Salsa

Chicken Wraps, *135*

Grilled Duck with Spicy Grapefruit, 90

Verde Pork Stew, *34*

Salsa Chicken Wraps, *135*

Salsa Verde Pork Stew, *34*

Saltimbocca Fennel and Orange Salad, 51

Sandwiches

Chicken Cubano Panini, 59

East-West Turkey Wraps, 77

French Dip, 11

Jamaican with Mango Mayonnaise, 85

Philly Cheese Steak, *121*

Salsa Chicken Wraps, *135*

Sweet Potato Falafel Sandwiches, *157*

Sauces

Beef in Tomato-Ginger Sauce, 28

Chicken Croquettes with Marinara, *61*

Negamaki with Ginger Dipping Sauce, *13*

Polenta with Tomato, *164*

Ravioli Bolognese, *104*

Spicy Cornish Hens with Mango, 84

Spicy Meatball Pitas with Yogurt Sauce, 73

Stuffed Bell Peppers with Tomato-Basil Sauce, 147

Sausage and Lentils, 82

Sausage and Polenta Ragoût, *74*

Sausage Shepherd's Pie, 41

Savory Baked Eggs, *165*

Savory Duck and Corn Salad, 89

Savory Slow-Cooker Meatloaf, 124

Savory Stuffed Acorn Squash, 49

Seafood

Chicken and Shrimp Tortilla Soup, 63

Rotini with Shrimp and Corn, 112

Turkey and Shrimp Gumbo, *141*

Turkey Tonnato, 139

Tuscan Pasta and Bean Salad with Tuna, *111*

Sesame Edamame Salad, *150*

Shrimp

and Chicken Tortilla Soup, 63

Rotini with Shrimp and Corn, 112

Turkey Gumbo and, *141*

Sicilian Meatball Soup, 107

Skillet Corn and Bean Chilaquiles, 173

Slow-Cooker Beef Chili, 122

Slow-Cooking

Asian-Style Pork Roast, 126

BBQ Turkey, *140*

Italian-Style Pot Roast, *120*

Mexicali Pork Stew, 130

Savory Slow-Cooker Meatloaf, 124

Slow-Cooker Beef Chili, 122

Smoky Bean and Ham Soup, *128*

Spanish Chicken and Rice, *134*

Spicy Chicken Stew, 136

Tropical Chicken, 132

Tuscan Braised Turkey, 138

Smoky Bean and Ham Soup, *128*

Smoky Beef Tacos, 22

Smoky Sausage and Potato Salad, 83

Soup

Beef-Noodle Soup Bowl, 95

Butternut Squash Soup, 174

Chicken and Shrimp Tortilla, 63

Double Soy, *151*

Greek Vegetable-Noodle Soup, 117

Italian Wedding Soup, *27*

Lentil Soup with Yogurt-Cilantro Topping, 163

Ravioli Minestrone, *105*

Roasted Beet and White Bean, 177

Roasted Corn Chowder, 172

Sicilian Meatball, 107

Smoky Bean and Ham Soup, *128*

Spicy Taco, 97

Thai Coconut, *99*

Wasabi Dumpling, *80*

Spaghetti and "Meatballs", 125

Spaghetti and Spinach Frittata, 109

Spaghetti Primavera with Sausage, 108

Spanish Chicken and Rice, *134*

Speedy Beef Fajitas, *19*

Spiced Steak with Onions and Peppers, 10

Spiced Three-Bean Stew, 158

Spicy Chicken Stew, 136

Spicy Cornish Hens with Mango Sauce, 84

Spicy Meatball Pitas with Yogurt Sauce, 73

Spicy Taco Soup, 97

Spinach

Spaghetti and Spinach Frittata, 109

Squash

Butternut Squash Soup, 174

Savory Stuffed Acorn, 49

Vegetable-Barley Risotto, 175

Stews

Beef Burgundy, 16

Hungarian Pepper with Noodles, 168

Lamb and Vegetable Stew, 46

Mexicali Pork, 130

Salsa Verde Pork, *34*

Spiced Three-Bean Stew, 158

Spicy Chicken, 136

Veal Stew Marsala, 48

Stuffed Bell Peppers with Tomato-Basil Sauce, 147

Sweet Potato and Chickpea Salad, *156*

Sweet Potato Falafel Sandwiches, *157*

T

Tacos

Smoky Beef, 22

Tandoori Beef Kebabs, 14

Tex-Mex Chili Pasta, 96

Tex-Mex Taco Salad, 123

Thai Chicken Salad, 65

Thai Coconut Soup, *99*

Thai Tofu and Vegetable Stir-Fry, *145*

Tofu

Balsamic Vegetable Salad and, 149

Lemony Caesar Salad, *144*

Thai Vegetable Stir-Fry and, *145*

Veggie Burgers, 146

Tomatoes

Beef in Tomato-Ginger Sauce, 28

Gnocchi with Parmesan and, *170*

Grape Tomato Clafouti, *171*

Polenta with Tomato Sauce, *164*

Savory Baked Eggs, *165*

Tortillas

Chicken and Shrimp Tortilla Soup, 63

East-West Turkey Wraps, 77

Pork and Rice Burritos, 131

Pork Tostadas, *35*

Salsa Chicken Wraps, *135*

Skillet Corn and Bean Chilaquiles, 173

Tostadas

Pork, *35*

Tropical Chicken, 132

Tuna Fish

Turkey Tonnato, 139

Tuscan Pasta and Bean Salad with, *111*

Turkey

Asian-Style Burgers, *81*

Baked Pasta and Meatballs, 106

BBQ, *140*

Crunchy Caesar Salad, 79

East-West Wraps, 77

Kiev Rolls, 78

Orange Roast, 76

Penne with Sausage and Broccoli, *110*

Sausage and Lentils, 82

Savory Slow-Cooker Meatloaf, 124

and Shrimp Gumbo, *141*

Sicilian Meatball Soup, 107

Smoky Sausage and Potato Salad, 83

Tonnato, 139

Tuscan Braised, 138

Wasabi Dumpling Soup, *80*

Turkey and Shrimp Gumbo, *141*

Turkey Kiev Rolls, 78

Turkey Tonnato, 139

Tuscan Braised Turkey, 138

Tuscan Pasta and Bean Salad with Tuna, *111*

V

Veal

Marsala Stew, 48

Old-Fashioned Meatloaf, *26*

Saltimbocca Fennel and Orange Salad, 51

Savory Stuffed Acorn Squash, 49

Veal Saltimbocca, 50

Veal Saltimbocca, 50

Veal Stew Marsala, 48

Vegetable-Barley Risotto, 175

Vegetables

Balsamic Vegetable and Tofu Salad, 149

Bell Pepper Tabbouleh Salad, 169

Butternut Squash Soup, 174

Cajun Bean Nachos, 159

Cannellini Beans and Swiss Chard with Ricotta, 154

Cauliflower Frittata, 167

Cheese Ravioli with Roasted Cauliflower, 166

Chickpea-Vegetable Salad, 153

Double Soy Soup, *151*

Easy Chickpea Curry, 152

Edamame-Zucchini Sauté, 148

Gnocchi with Tomato and Parmesan, *170*

Grape Tomato Clafouti, *171*

Greek Vegetable-Noodle Soup, 117

Hungarian Pepper Stew with Noodles, 168

Lemon-Honey Beans and Carrots, 160

Lemony Tofu Caesar Salad, *144*

Lentil Soup with Yogurt-Cilantro Topping, 163

Middle Eastern-Style Lentils and Rice, 162

Polenta with Tomato Sauce, *164*

Quinoa with Swiss Chard and Almonds, 155

Raspberry Wild Rice and Bean Salad, 161

Roasted Beet and Goat Cheese Salad with Mint, 176

Roasted Beet and White Bean Soup, 177

Roasted Corn Chowder, 172

Roasted Feta Pasta and, 116

Savory Stuffed Acorn Squash, 49

Skillet Corn and Bean Chilaquiles, 173

Spiced Three-Bean Stew, 158

Stuffed Bell Peppers with Tomato-Basil Sauce, 147

Sweet Potato and Chickpea Salad, *156*

Sweet Potato Falafel Sandwiches, *157*

Thai Tofu Stir-Fry and, *145*

Vegetable-Barley Risotto, 175

Veggie Tofu Burgers, 146

Veggie Tofu Burgers, 146

Vietnamese Chicken Curry, 64

W

Wasabi Dumpling Soup, *80*

Wine

Veal Stew Marsala, 48

Wraps

East-West Turkey, 77

Salsa Chicken, *135*

Y

Yogurt

Lemony Pork and Lentil Salad, 37

Lentil Soup with Yogurt-Cilantro Topping, 163

Spicy Meatball Pitas with Yogurt Sauce, 73

Z

Zucchini

Edamame Sauté, 148

Recipes by *POINTS* value

1 *POINTS* value

Balsamic Vegetable and Tofu Salad, 149

Butternut Squash Soup, 174

2 *POINTS* value

Cauliflower Frittata, 167

Grape Tomato Clafouti, 171

Savory Baked Eggs, 165

3 *POINTS* value

Bell Pepper Tabbouleh Salad, 169

Chicken Egg Foo Yung, 69

Chili con Pollo, 70

Crunchy Turkey Caesar Salad, 79

Double Soy Soup, 151

Lentil Soup with Yogurt-Cilantro Topping, 163

Roasted Beet and Goat Cheese Salad with Mint, 176

Veal Saltimbocca, 50

4 *POINTS* value

Asian-Style Grilled Flank Steak, 12

Balsamic Sausage and Peppers, 40

Buffalo Chicken Salad, 133

Caribbean Cornish Hen and Sweet Potato Salad, 87

Chicken and Shrimp Tortilla Soup, 63

Chimichurri Pepper Steak, 18

Chipotle Roast Pork, 32

Duck with Brandied Cherries, 88

Ham and Apple Slaw, 43

Ham with Fresh Peach Chutney, 42

Korean Beef in Lettuce Cups, 25

Lemon-Honey Beans and Carrots, 160

Mango-Glazed Drumsticks, 68

Orange Roast Turkey, 76

Polenta with Tomato Sauce, 164

Raspberry Wild Rice and Bean Salad, 161

Roast Chicken with Lemon and Oregano, 54

Roasted Beet and White Bean Soup, 177

Roasted Corn Chowder, 172

Roasted Vegetable-Feta Pasta, 116

Savory Duck and Corn Salad, 89

Spiced Steak with Onions and Peppers, 10

Spicy Chicken Stew, 136

Sweet Potato and Chickpea Salad, 156

Tandoori Beef Kebabs, 14

Thai Coconut Soup, 99

Turkey Kiev Rolls, 78

Turkey Tonnato, 139

Vegetable-Barley Risotto, 175

Veggie Tofu Burgers, 146

Wasabi Dumpling Soup, 80

5 *POINTS* value

Apricot-Glazed Chicken, 58

Beef-Noodle Soup Bowl, 95

Chicken Fried Rice, 137

Chicken Marengo, 56

Chicken with Olives and Artichokes, 60

Chickpea-Vegetable Salad, 153

Double Chili Pork Roast, 30

East-West Turkey Wraps, 77

Edamame-Zucchini Sauté, 148

French Dip Sandwiches, 11

Gnocchi with Tomato and Parmesan, 170

Greek Vegetable-Noodle Soup, 117

Grilled Duck with Spicy Grapefruit Salsa, 90

Hungarian Pepper Stew with Noodles, 168

Jamaican Sandwiches with Mango Mayonnaise, 85

Lebanese Pita Pizzas, 29

Lemony Tofu Caesar Salad, 144

Linguine with Asparagus and Ricotta, 114

Middle-Eastern Chicken, 66

Negamaki with Ginger Dipping Sauce, 13

Orange-Glazed Pork Chops with Fennel, 36

Pressure-Cooker Corned Beef, 20

Saltimbocca Fennel and Orange Salad, 51

Savory Slow-Cooker Meatloaf, 124

Sicilian Meatball Soup, 107

Skillet Corn and Bean Chilaquiles, 173

Smoky Sausage and Potato Salad, 83

Spaghetti and Spinach Frittata, 109

Spiced Three-Bean Stew, 158

Spicy Cornish Hens with Mango Sauce, 84

Spicy Meatball Pitas with Yogurt Sauce, 73

Thai Chicken Salad, 65

Thai Tofu and Vegetable Stir-Fry, 145

Turkey and Shrimp Gumbo, 141

Tuscan Braised Turkey, 138

Tuscan Pasta and Bean Salad with Tuna, 111

6 *POINTS* value

Asian-Style Burgers, 81

Baked Pasta and Meatballs, 106

Cajun Bean Nachos, 159

Cannellini Beans and Swiss Chard with Ricotta, 154

Chicken and Asparagus Risotto, 57

Chicken Cubano Panini, 59

Chicken Waldorf Salad, 55

Corned Beef Hash, 21

Cornish Hens with Apples, 86

Duck Hash, 91

Farfalle with Sausage, Fennel, and Peppers, 75

Hoisin Burgers, 24

Italian Wedding Soup, 27

Lamb and Vegetable Stew, 46

Lamb Tagine with Apricots, 45

Mac 'n' Cheese Cakes with Greens and Ham, 103

Mexican Pork and Veggie Bake, 33

Miso-Glazed Pork, 38

Pork Tostadas, 35

Roast Lamb with Bulgur and Mint Pesto, 44

Rotini with Shrimp and Corn, 112

Sausage and Polenta Ragoût, 74

Sausage Shepherd's Pie, 41

Savory Stuffed Acorn Squash, 49

Sesame Edamame Salad, 150

Spaghetti and "Meatballs", 125

Sweet Potato Falafel Sandwiches, 157

Tex-Mex Chili Pasta, 96

Tex-Mex Taco Salad, 123

Tropical Chicken, 132

Vietnamese Chicken Curry, 64

7 POINTS value

Argentinean-Style Chicken, 62

Beef and Bean Sloppy Joes, 23

Beef Burgundy Stew, 16

Beef in Tomato-Ginger Sauce, 28

Beef Stroganoff, 17

Cheese Ravioli with Roasted Cauliflower, 166

Chicken Croquettes with Marinara Sauce, 61

Chicken Mac 'n' Cheese, 102

Chicken Samosas with Mango Chutney, 67

Chinese Pork and Noodles, 98

Easy Cassoulet, 129

Hoisin Noodles with Beef and Broccoli, 94

Hunan Pork and Peppers, 127

Italian-Style Pot Roast, 120

Lamb-Noodle Casserole, 47

Lemony Pork and Lentil Salad, 37

Mexicali Pork Stew, 130

Moroccan Meatballs with Couscous, 72

Old-Fashioned Meatloaf, 26

Penne with Sausage and Broccoli, 110

Pork and Bok Choy Noodle Bowl, 31

Pork and Rice Burritos, 131

Pork Fried Rice, 39

Ravioli Minestrone, 105

Salsa Verde Pork Stew, 34

Sausage and Lentils, 82

Slow-Cooker Beef Chili, 122

Smoky Bean and Ham Soup, 128

Smoky Beef Tacos, 22

Spaghetti Primavera with Sausage, 108

Speedy Beef Fajitas, 19

Spicy Taco Soup, 97

Stuffed Bell Peppers with Tomato-Basil Sauce, 147

Veal Stew Marsala, 48

8 POINTS value

Baked Pasta e Fagioli, 113

BBQ Turkey, 140

Braised Chicken and Couscous, 100

Chicken and Penne Casserole, 71

Chicken-Couscous Salad, 101

Easy Beef Curry, 15

Easy Chickpea Curry, 152

Middle Eastern-Style Lentils and Rice, 162

Pasta "Pizza", 115

Philly Cheese Steak Sandwiches, 121

Quinoa with Swiss Chard and Almonds, 155

Ravioli Bolognese, 104

Salsa Chicken Wraps, 135

9 POINTS value

Asian-Style Pork Roast, 126

Spanish Chicken and Rice, 134

Recipes that work with the Simply Filling technique

Argentinean-Style Chicken, 62

Bell Pepper Tabbouleh Salad, 169

Butternut Squash Soup, 174

Cauliflower Frittata, 167

Chicken Fried Rice, 137

Chicken with Olives and Artichokes, 60

Chickpea-Vegetable Salad, 153

Chimichurri Pepper Steak, 18

Easy Chickpea Curry, 152

Hungarian Pepper Stew with Noodles, 168

Mexicali Pork Stew, 130

Orange Roast Turkey, 76

Roast Chicken with Lemon and
Oregano, 54

Roasted Beet and White Bean Soup, 177

Rotini with Shrimp and Corn, 112

Savory Baked Eggs, 165

Savory Duck and Corn Salad, 89

Spiced Steak with Onions and Peppers, 10

Tandoori Beef Kebabs, 14

Turkey Tonnato, 139

Tuscan Braised Turkey, 138

Notes